Welcome

PECO
MODELLERS' LIBRARY

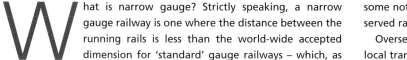

Your Guide to
MODELLING NARROW GAUGE RAILWAYS

What is narrow gauge? Strictly speaking, a narrow gauge railway is one where the distance between the running rails is less than the world-wide accepted dimension for 'standard' gauge railways – which, as we all know, is a distance of 4'8½" (1435mm).

In the British Isles, narrow gauge was typically used for relatively short lines, often built when the expense of a standard gauge branch could not be justified, either due to the difficulty of the terrain or the marginal projected patronage. Main costs were kept down through economies in civil engineering, and lines frequently served a single purpose: to link a remote source of minerals or an industrial site with a shipping port or the nearest standard gauge railhead. The development of agriculture and (much later) tourism were also important factors that led to narrow gauge being employed wherever and whenever the need arose.

Narrow gauge railway building reached a peak between the turn of the 20th century and WW1; there was a brief revival during those war years, and renewed interest in some quarters thereafter with the availability of cheap surplus material which had been built for military purposes during the conflict. However, this late flowering was short-lived and most lines had disappeared by the start of WW2. There were some notable exceptions, and we should not forget that the first preserved railway, the Talyllyn, is narrow gauge.

Overseas, on all continents, narrow gauge was employed both for local transportation applications, such as mining and minerals, timber, sugar plantations, etc., and also significantly as trunk routes with larger colonial and Continental systems of 3'6" or metre gauge whose function, operation, and resulting character, made them essentially main line networks. Although there is considerable commercial support for Continental metre gauge (though oddly, hardly any for colonial subjects), these networks are too large to include other than a passing reference in this book even though they technically fit the description of narrow gauge.

Narrow gauge railways have been a popular topic for modelling in both the UK and overseas for many decades, and whilst they may not, at first, appear to have the majesty and exhilaration of full size main line railways, I believe that what you shall discover within the pages of this book will fundamentally change your mind and outlook, and you'll be hooked on the delights, freedoms and fulfilment that narrow gauge modelling – in all its guises – can truly bring.

Steve Flint
Editor and photographer

Standard gauge and narrow gauge side by side at Welshpool in 1963. Both locomotives are built to the same nominal 'scale' (ie 1:1 full size) but the standard gauge 14xx 0-4-2T on the left is significantly larger all round than *The Earl*, one of the 2'6" gauge machines of the Welshpool & Llanfair Light Railway.
Photo: Colour-Rail

Editor & Photographer
Steve Flint

Production Editor
Tim Rayner

Contributors
Steve Flint, Tim Rayner, Craig Tiley,
Andrew Burnham, David Malton,
Andrew & Joseph Beard,
Bob Phelps

Editorial Assistant
Julie Newbery

Art Director
Adrian Stickland

Review Photographer
Jolyon Sargent

Graphic Illustration
Brian Meredith, Dave Clements,
Gary Bickley

General & Advertisement Manager
John King

Advertisement Assistant
Sue Davis

Classified Advertisements
Nicole Charlton

Direct Subscriptions
Alicia Knight

Editorial Director
C M Pritchard

Editorial Office Telephone
01297 20580

ISBN 505-0881097595

Distribution to the model trade, direct subscriptions
(Home & Overseas) Pritchard Patent Product Co Ltd
(address and telephone as below).

Distribution to the newsagency trade (Home &
Overseas) Marketforce (UK), Second Floor,
5 Churchill Place, Canary Wharf, London E14 5HU.

Printed by
Acanthus Press Ltd,
Unit 21, Ryelands Business Park, Bagley Road,
Wellington, Somerset TA21 9PZ.

Peco Publications & Publicity Ltd,
Beer, Seaton, Devon, EX12 3NA, England.
Telephone: 01297 20580 Fax 01297 20229
Website: www.pecopublications.co.uk
Email: railway-modeller@btconnect.com

Contents

27

88

96

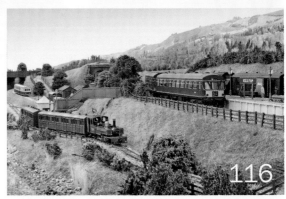

116

Chapter 1

The delights of narrow gauge railway modelling

Above
Welsh narrow gauge then – Western Region (Vale of Rheidol) No.8 nearing Devils Bridge with the 2.30pm from Aberystwyth on 16 August 1951.
Photo:
Hugh Ballantyne/ Rail Photoprints

Left
Welsh narrow gauge now – the rebuilt Welsh Highland Railway uses ex-South African NGG16 Garratts to haul trains through some spectacular scenery. No.138 approaches the road crossing at Pont Croesor on 12 September 2010.
Photo:
Graham Lightfoot

W hy, when there is such a marvellous abundance of ready-to-run standard gauge model railway equipment in N, OO and O gauge, would anyone choose to model a narrow gauge railway?

There isn't a simple answer, but for as long as the hobby has been around, many hundreds of modellers have forsaken the power, glamour and excitement of standard gauge trains to derive, instead, much enjoyment and pleasure from the delights of narrow gauge modelling.

The world over, narrow gauge railways are fascinating systems. They often ran through scenically beautiful areas, operating typically short trains on lines with very sharp curves – features and aspects that are ideally suited to rep-

resentation in model form, especially so when space for the railway is at a premium.

Many may perhaps be familiar with narrow gauge lines known collectively as the Great Little Trains of Wales, which includes the oldest heritage railway in the UK – The Talyllyn Railway, which in 2015 celebrated its 150th anniversary. This, and others in the group such as the Ffestiniog, Welsh Highland and Corris railways, started out as mineral lines, subsequently carrying passengers, and were all preserved or reconstructed by volunteer organisations to operate as tourist lines.

It only takes a journey on any of those lines to see why they can be so fascinating and inspiring. Moreover, they are survivors from a time when narrow gauge railways

were more widespread in the UK. Lines such as the Lynton & Barnstaple, the Leek & Manifold, the Ashover, the Glyn Valley, the Campbeltown & Machrihanish, the Southwold – and many more – existed as complete freight and passenger operations in their own right. They are all now defunct but serve as prototypical inspiration of narrow gauge railways as they really were. Efforts to reconstruct aspects of some of those long-gone lines are underway, and happily historical documentry evidence and photographs exist, providing sufficient material for modellers.

It is perhaps the Lynton & Barnstaple Railway which embodies the spirit of historical British narrow gauge more than any other line. Sufficient, it seems, to persuade Peco to produce the exquisite OO9 coach and wagon models which were released in 2014 in anticipation of ready-to-run 009 locomotives.

There was, and still is, much more to British narrow gauge railways than the Welsh tourist lines and the aforementioned much lamented historical routes. Quarries, clay pits, brickworks, mineral mines, stately estates, potato farms and countless other establishments could all boast their own narrow gauge railway system. They could be ramshackle affairs, or well organised and maintained, but

they all had a special kind of curious charm and atmosphere – perfect for the modeller seeking something a little bit different, and many are examined in more detail in the next chapter.

Beyond our shores, narrow gauge railways could be found in a greater abundance. Ireland for instance had several systems, often to a bigger loading gauge than their counterparts on the mainland. Further afield still, to continental Europe, America and the rest of the world, narrow gauge railway systems could be found everywhere; mining, logging, sugar plantations, mountainous terrain. Many of these are examined in Chapter 3 which, along with the British and Irish systems should prove that power, glamour and excitement can be also be found on narrow gauge railways!

Free from standard patterns and practices

When building a standard gauge layout, modellers seeking accuracy and authenticity are constrained by the standard pattern and practices of the railways concerned, be that British Railways, one of the Big Four companies, or any of the pre-Grouping railways. You know the sort of aspects; architectural style, signalling systems, etc. Narrow gauge

Top left
One of the small Hunslets, George B, that were synonymous with Dinorwic Quarry in North Wales for many years, hard at work in June 1961.
Photo: Ron Fisher

Above
On the 750mm gauge Fichtelbergbahn in East Germany, standard 2-10-2T No.99 1778-2 is seen climbing between Hammerunterwiesenthal and the terminus at Oberwiesenthal on 22 August 1983. The line here runs very close to the border and the hills in the background are in Czechoslovakia.
Photo: Frank Hornby

Below
A train on the Nocton Estate railway poses for the camera at a road crossing between Lincoln and Sleaford in 1932.
Photo: Ray Hooley, reproduced by kind permission of the Oakwood Press

Above
Going freelance frees you up from the constraints imposed when modelling a standard gauge line or prototype narrow gauge railway. The modeller is free to choose his own locomotive and stock designs, and select liveries and logos to suit, as exemplified by Daniel James Wells' *Llanrhyn and Porthnewydd Railway.*

modelling – unless you want to replicate a real place or station accurately – generally frees you from those rigid style and design constraints: you decide for yourself the standards and operating practices on your own railway. This is an approach which is known as freelancing; you choose the signals, the locomotive types, the architecture, and so on, and create an individual and unique railway that no one can criticise or say is wrong!

Another consideration is that, unlike a large main line system, it is feasible to recreate – or at least have a reasonable attempt at representing – a full narrow gauge line from end to end, complete with its locomotive and stock designs and unique liveries.

This approach, and the nature of narrow gauge history, also means that the fictional might-have-been lines, so favoured by modellers are easier to justify, and throughout the lifespan of the hobby many modellers have created just such compelling and believable railways, as we shall examine later in this chapter.

Small space

The problems faced by all railway modellers when trying to compress an ideal layout into the available space tend to be less with narrow gauge lines, as their installations and track configurations were more modest in real life. The economical sharp curves and steep gradients favoured by their original engineers will be welcome to the space-starved modeller. Furthermore, narrow locos tend to be smaller and the trains generally shorter. Narrow gauge railways are therefore ideal for modelling in limited spaces, but not exclusively so, as we shall discover.

Right
Dean Hill in OO9 by Jim & Lyn Owers packs a lot of narrow gauge railway into a small space. It depicts the former Royal Navy Armaments Depot of the same name which operated until 2004.
Photo: Jim Owers

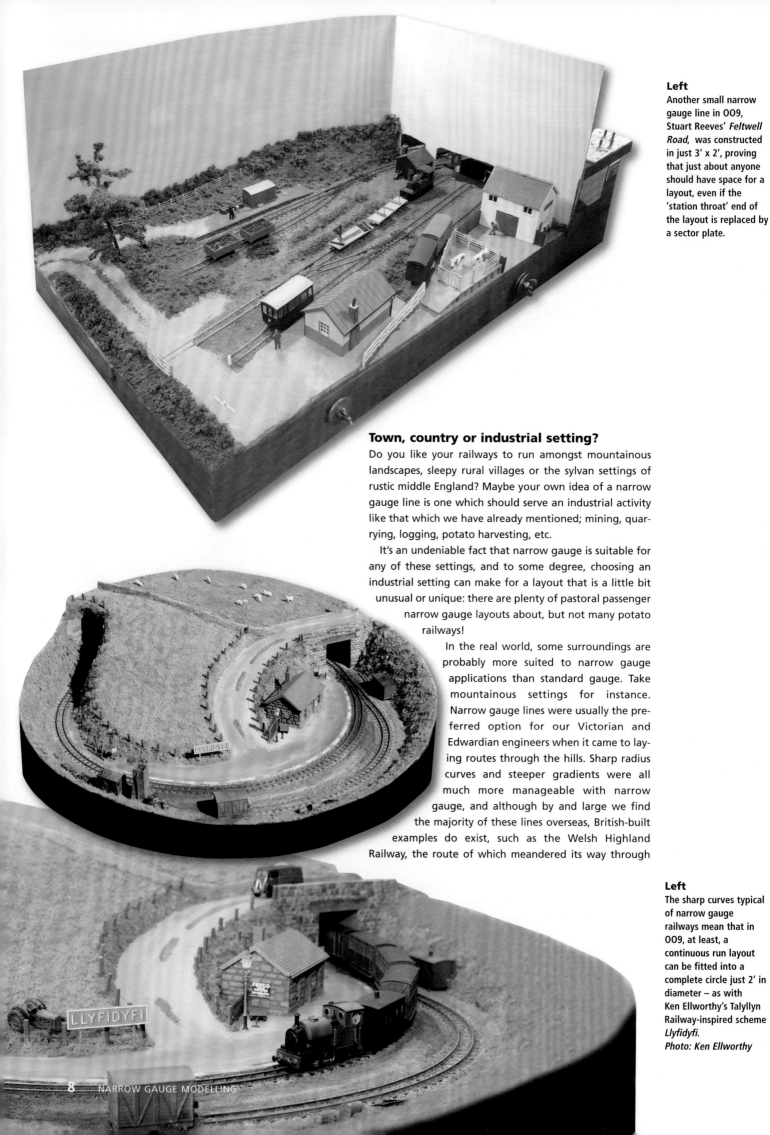

Town, country or industrial setting?

Do you like your railways to run amongst mountainous landscapes, sleepy rural villages or the sylvan settings of rustic middle England? Maybe your own idea of a narrow gauge line is one which should serve an industrial activity like that which we have already mentioned; mining, quarrying, logging, potato harvesting, etc.

It's an undeniable fact that narrow gauge is suitable for any of these settings, and to some degree, choosing an industrial setting can make for a layout that is a little bit unusual or unique: there are plenty of pastoral passenger narrow gauge layouts about, but not many potato railways!

In the real world, some surroundings are probably more suited to narrow gauge applications than standard gauge. Take mountainous settings for instance. Narrow gauge lines were usually the preferred option for our Victorian and Edwardian engineers when it came to laying routes through the hills. Sharp radius curves and steeper gradients were all much more manageable with narrow gauge, and although by and large we find the majority of these lines overseas, British-built examples do exist, such as the Welsh Highland Railway, the route of which meandered its way through

Left
The sharp curves typical of narrow gauge railways mean that in OO9, at least, a continuous run layout can be fitted into a complete circle just 2' in diameter – as with Ken Ellworthy's Talyllyn Railway-inspired scheme *Llyfidyfi*.
Photo: Ken Ellworthy

the Snowdonian foothills and happily has now been reopened throughout for the benefit of railway enthusiasts and tourists alike.

Rural England of course, provides the setting for countless thousands of layouts in all scales and gauges, so it's no wonder that many narrow gaugers choose it. Combining a rural industry with passenger services can be a useful way of adding a bit of extra interest and operating potential, but in the final analysis, it's your railway and if you adopt the freelance approach you can really do as you think fit.

Right
Green End by David Gander is a OO9 layout which occupies a length of just 7' including the fiddle yard. The width is only 10", and David suggests that this ratio of length to width creates the illusion that the layout is much longer than it is.
Photo: David Gander

Below
Small layouts are also practical in O-16.5 gauge – 7mm scale models running on 16.5mm gauge track. This one, *Langney End*, was built by James Williams and was contained in an area of 10' x 2'.

Above
Streetside running in Ireland at Hollyhill on the Schull & Skibbereen Railway in this classic scene, captured in July 1938. The loco is S&S No.4, formerly named *Erin* and built by Nasmyth Wilson in 1888.
Photo: H C Casserley

Below
Former East German streetside running; 2-8-2T No.99 2323-6 on the 900mm gauge 'Molli', built to take tourists between the standard gauge station in Bad Doberan and the Baltic coast.
Photo: Graham Lightfoot

Porthmadog, in Gwynedd, where the reborn Welsh Highland Railway runs along tracks embedded in tarmac to gain access to Ffestiniog Railway metals at Harbour station.

Quirky

Narrow gauge model railways serve quarries, clay pits, estates and even treacle mines! Yes, there was even a OO9 layout called *The Barley Sugar Line*, built and exhibited by the Burnley Model Railway Club, inspired by folklore concerning the supposed treacle mines of Sabden in Lancashire. So quirky – if we can use that word without upsetting anyone – is also a subject category that has been exploited by a few narrow gauge layout builders over the years, all with the aim to instil a little novelty and mirth into the hobby, reminding certain breeds of modeller that we shouldn't take ourselves too seriously.

One genre of the novelty layout was the so-called 'rabbit warren' railway, where the train would disappear into a tunnel only to re-emerge on the other side of the layout, and at a different level, and travelling in the opposite direction. These proved popular back in the pioneering days of OO9 in the 1960s, but are largely a thing of the past, as some might be relieved to hear. Such arrangements are not inherently bad, and can even mimic certain prototype situations, but they do tend to present narrow gauge as a caricature to exploit the potential of sharp curves and steep gradients to an absurd degree.

Serious modellers should look away now, lest they feel offended, but time and again idiosyncratic layouts such as these picked up the best in show public vote at exhibitions. *Llandoug*, a rabbit warren-style layout with plenty of

Towns and cities, at least in the British Isles, rarely sported a narrow gauge line. Smaller towns, yes, such as Southwold, Barnstaple and Leek were served by narrow gauge stations. Campbelltown in Scotland and Hollyhill in Ireland had narrow gauge lines running through the streets, though again you generally have to visit overseas locations to find narrow gauge routes running streetside through the town . One such exception in this country is at

Above
The modern-day Welsh Highland Railway includes a few short sections of street operation, although here it is treated as a level crossing to keep road traffic out of the way. Former South African Garratt No.87 eases its passenger train into Porthmadog Harbour station on the evening of 29 April 2011.
Photo:
Andrew Burnham

Right
The Burnley Model Railway Club's OO9 layout *The Barley Sugar Line* (see RM November 1995), was inspired by the mythological treacle mines of Sabden in Lancashire.

animated effects, built by the late Doug Metcalfe, was seen on the northern exhibition circuit in the 1980s in the days when smoking was allowed indoors. Doug would blow his cigarette smoke into a plastic tube at the back of the layout and all the chimneys on the layout would come to life! Fears about passive smoking didn't prevent him winning the public vote on several occasions! Sadly as far as the authors are aware, no photos of Neil and Doug's work exist.

Rabbit warren-style layouts still do appear on the circuit even to this day, and although smoking chimneys are produced using much healthier alternatives, such layouts can still be very entertaining: for example, Jim & Lyn Owers' *Dolfriog*, which actually encompasses several different narrow gauges – but no smoking chimneys – is a case in point.

Other sources of inspiration for the unusual and off-beat have also been exploited. Classic written works by J R R Tolkien and Terry Pratchett spring to mind, for instance, Hugh Norwood built a model of a station which might have existed in Pratchett's *Discworld* which he called *Angst-Lesspork*. Quirky perhaps, but skilfully executed, definitely. Rowland Emett-inspired railways have also been built, such as the 1970s-era *Far Twittering and Oysterperch Railway*, and more recently, Matt Wildsmith's whimsical

Lumpy Barmcake & Salted Cracker Railway, which also drew inspiration from children's favourites *Camberwick Green* and *Wallace and Gromit*.

Something for everyone

By now you will hopefully share our view that narrow gauge railway modelling can offer plenty of scope and variety, albeit devoid of those great and powerful main line steam or diesel engines which captivated and enthralled us in our youth, but if you want big and powerful, then take a look at overseas narrow gauge lines outlined in Chapter 4.

That said, railway modelling doesn't always have to be about glamorous locomotives and roaring express trains, other considerations like a shortage of space, or a limited budget, may be sufficient to sway you into considering a narrow gauge layout as a serious alternative to trying to squeeze 10-coach trains into a 8' x 6' spare room.

The key advantages are that you can get away with tighter radius curves and steeper gradients than with the equivalent in standard gauge, whatever narrow gauge modelling scale you choose – and that brings us nicely to the topic of which scale/gauge ratio you should consider for your project.

Above
Layouts built in the 'Rabbit Warren' style are very entertaining for the general public. Jim & Lyn Owers' *Dolfriog*, which has several different gauge sections, is a latter day example of the genre.
Photo: Jim Owers

Right
Hugh Norwood's layout, based on the *Discworld* fantasy novels written by Terry Pratchett, shows that adopting an unusual setting can still be a challenging and exacting modelling proposition.

Below
Matt Wildsmith took a break from the exacting standards of finescale modelling to produce this Emmett style layout which he called the *Lumpy Barmcake & Salted Cracker Railway* – a take on the LB&SCR.

Question of scale

Ask a model railway enthusiast to name a narrow gauge railway scale and invariably they will mention OO9. This is because OO9 has been the most popular scale/gauge ratio in the UK for over half a century. It represents 4mm scale model locos and stock which run on 9mm gauge track. Typically that represents a prototype gauge of 2'3" as used by The Talyllyn Railway (www.talyllyn.co.uk), but for all intents and purposes many narrow gauge devotees are happy to use OO9 to depict any narrow gauge prototype of between 2' and 3'. Yes, there are modellers who want to stick rigidly to the correct scale/gauge ratio – and that's their prerogative, but in many ways, a ready acceptance of a modest compromise such as this makes narrow gauge modelling all the more appealing. Moreover there is a lot of commercial support for OO9 both here and overseas (it is known abroad as HOe) so getting started in the gauge can be relatively straightforward.

However, there is a huge range of scale/gauge ratios from which potential narrow gauge modellers can choose. The most well known are listed in table 1. At first glance the list may seem confusing and complicated as different modelling scales are linked to lots of different track gauges, some of which are commercially available, others not.

These scale/gauge ratios have evolved over the years because innovative modellers have been canny in making use of ready-to-run motor/chassis units from one scale on which they scratchbuild loco bodies in the chosen narrow gauge scale. For example, the use of N gauge mechanisms which run on 9mm gauge track are used to create 4mm/ft scale locos and stock: resulting in OO9 models. Another popular example is using OO gauge mechanisms (which run on 16.5mm gauge track) to create locos built to

Above
There is a myriad of combinations of scale and gauge in narrow gauge railway modelling. In the UK the most popular is OO9, followed closely by O-16.5, for indoor railways. *Bryn-Dinas* (above) is an example of O9, a less common modelling size which uses 7mm scale models on 9mm gauge track, representing approximately a 15" gauge prototype railway. Our continental and American modelling friends have even more scale gauge combinations from which to choose, and for the outdoor narrow gauge enthusiast, there is SM32 and G scale of which you can read more about in Chapter 5 on page 96. *Bryn-Dinas* was part of the *Ceriog Valley Railway* system, built by Brian Fryer.

7mm/ft scale: the result is O-16.5 models. The list in the table goes on, and some modellers have even invented their own. Historically, when TT gauge mechanisms were available off the shelf, many, such as the legendary P D Hancock, adapted them to create true 3' gauge railway depictions – ie 4mm/ft scale on TT (12mm gauge) track known as OOn3. 12mm gauge track is still commercially available in the guise of Peco HOm, but mechanisms either have to be hand-made or adapted from continental TT gauge ready-to-run models.

To summarise, the myriad of narrow gauge scale/gauge ratios seen in Table 1 has evolved principally because of the initial inventiveness of individual modellers being followed, eventually, by the manufacturers producing appropriate equipment.

Ready-to-run equipment

If you have experience with standard gauge model railways, either in N gauge, OO gauge, or even O gauge, you will be aware of the fantastic support given to these sizes of model railway equipment by the various manufacturers. Sadly narrow gauge is, relatively speaking, very poorly supported by manufacturers in the UK. Overseas is much different, with numerous European, American and Far

Table 1 – narrow gauge scale/gauge combinations

Common description	Scale	(to ft)	Gauge	Prototype depicted
British				
Nn3	1:148	2.1mm	6.5mm (Z)	3'
TTn3	1:100	3mm	9mm (N)	3'
OO6.5	1:76	4mm	6.5mm (Z)	1'6"
OO9	1:76	4mm	9mm (N)	1'10" to 2'6"
OOn3	1:76	4mm	12mm (TT)	3'
5.5mm	1:55	5.5mm	12mm (TT)	2'
O-9	1:43.5	7mm	9mm (N)	'3" to 1'6"
O-16.5	1:43.5	7mm	16.5mm (OO)	1'10" to 2'6"
On2	1:48	¼"	½" (12.5mm)	2'
On30	1:48	¼"	16.5mm (OO)	2'6"
On3	1:48	¼"	¾" (19mm)	3'
9 mill	1:34	9mm	32mm (O)	3'6" (New Zealand)
G	1:24	½"	45mm (1)	3'
SM32	1:19	16mm	32mm (O)	2'
Continental				
Nm	1:160	2mm	6.5mm (Z)	metre
HOf	1:87	3.5mm	6.5mm (Z)	600mm Feldbahn
HOe	1:87	3.5mm	9mm (N)	750/760mm
HOm	1:87	3.5mm	12mm (TT)	metre
Oe	1:45	7mm	16.5mm (HO)	750/760mm
Om	1:45	7mm	22.5mm	metre
Ie	1:32	9.5mm	23.5mm	750/760mm
Im	1:32	9.5mm	32mm (O)	metre
IIe	1:22.5	13.5mm	30/32mm	600 to 760mm
IIm	1:22.5	13.5mm	45mm (1)	metre
American				
Nn3	1:160	2mm	6.5mm (Z)	3'
HOn2½/HOn30	1:87	3.5mm	9mm (N)	2'6" and 2'
HOn3	1:87	3.5mm	10.5mm	3'
Sn3	1:64	³⁄₁₆"	⁹⁄₁₆" (14.5mm)	3'
Sn3½	1:64	³⁄₁₆"	16.5mm (HO)	3'6" (New Zealand, South Africa)
On2	1:48	¼"	½" (12.5mm)	2'
On30	1:48	¼"	16.5mm (HO)	2'6"
On3	1:48	¼"	¾" (19mm)	3'
G	1:24	½"	45mm (1)	3'

Left

When it comes to creating locomotives, narrow gauge modellers in the smaller scales have had to be innovative for quite some time, building engine bodies by scratch or adapting plastic kits and mounting them on ready-to-run chassis from the major manufacturers. Things are set to change however in OO9: Bachmann is developing a War Department Baldwin 4-6-0T and associated rolling stock (some of which was brought to the market in late 2017), and the Manning Wardle 2-6-2Ts of the Lynton & Barnstaple Railway are available from Heljan. The latter complement the range of L&B coaches and wagons already available from Peco.

Eastern brands providing a swathe of interesting models of which more information appears on page 86. The UK is finally catching up, in OO9 at least, thanks to the efforts of Peco which is producing a growing range of ready-to-run carriages and wagons, and mainstream manufacturers Heljan releasing its L&B 2-6-2T in 2017, and Bachmann likely to deliver its WDLR models soon after.

The world's largest small scale narrow gauge modelling association

In the RAILWAY MODELLER for September 1973, a notice appeared asking if anyone was interested in forming an 'OO9 Gauge Society'. From the original handful of members, the Society has grown to an international group of around 1,600 and celebrated its 40th Anniversary in 2013 with a hugely successful weekend Convention in Kegworth, Leicestershire.

The Society's aim is to support and facilitate narrow gauge modelling in 3.5mm and 4mm scales across a range of narrow gauges – primarily from 6mm to 12mm gauge, although the main focus is generally on 9mm gauge for OO9 and HOe.

The Society offers a number of benefits to members. From a double sided, single page newsletter back in 1973, we now produce a monthly, full colour, 24 page magazine featuring news, reviews, and articles. Alongside this, our Members' Sales department continues to provide members with access to a wide range of previously owned models and other items, including those often hard to find chassis! It is a familiar and popular stand at the many narrow gauge modelling events throughout the year.

In recent times a number of members' exclusive kits have been introduced. The Hudson Toastrack coach, Irish cattle van and Royal Naval Armaments rolling stock have proved popular, and we intend to continue to

grow this range over the years to come as part of our ambition to give members something that can't be found elsewhere.

Many members enjoy the social side of railway modelling and a number of local area groups have been formed who meet regularly to exchange ideas and enjoy OO9 modelling with like minded individuals. There are 20 groups across the country (plus one in the Netherlands!). Several of our groups hold Members' Days – mini exhibitions with a handful of layouts and perhaps one or two traders where members can get together to

enjoy their hobby in a casual environment. In fact you will find our calendar now features an event of this nature on almost a monthly basis, across the country.

As well as the welcome arrival of ready to run rolling stock in OO9 from Peco, the new range of locomotives from Fourdees, and the promise of more to come from Heljan and Bachmann, the 009 Society is also mindful of its heritage. Over the years, the Society has become home to a number of models produced by the pioneers in our scale, including P D Hancock, Derek Naylor and David Mander. We also have a small but growing archive of documents and ephemera connected with OO9 modelling and the Society.

With our growing membership and social events, and the new interest from established manufacturers, it really feels as if OO9 modelling is enjoying a surge in popularity. There is also growing support from smaller traders, who are using new techniques such as 3D printing to open up the market and make it

possible to combine a personal modelling interest with small runs of interesting kits and products.

If you would like to join us, details of membership can be found on our website www.009society.com or via our Membership Secretary, The 009 Society, 70 Grove Road, Shirley, Southampton, Hampshire SO15 3GG.

David Gander
Chairman, 009 Society

Members' Day events are organised by area groups, such as this, at Barton-le-Clay, Bedfordshire. *Photos: Mick Thornton or as credited*

Modelling demonstrations by members; Martin Collins and Michael Campbell of the Sussex Downs Group showcase the Society at ExpoNG. *Photo: Tom Dauben*

Chapter 2

Narrow gauge adventures

A journey of discovery

Despite the general paucity of ready-to-run models over the years, narrow gauge modelling has been very popular within the UK hobby for a long time. So let's take a look at some of those inventive modellers who have influenced and inspired the growth and interest of narrow gauge railway modelling. Where it all began is debatable, so we will begin by looking at some classic layouts that depict complete narrow gauge systems.

One of the first pioneers of this genre was the late P D Hancock, who dreamt up and created the *Craig and Mertonford Railway* back in the 1950s. What Hancock did was not only build a fine layout, but he was one of the first to create a complete fictional history for his railway, create personae for the would-be staff of the line, devise timetables and generate freight flows, and document workshop visits for his locomotives and stock. It was a complete railway world of fiction recreated in miniature and in some ways, that all embracing scenario is what makes narrow gauge railway modelling so engaging. A world of our own in which we can become absorbed in much the same way as we would a novel, a play or movie.

Hancock's *modus operandi* became a template which countless other modellers have since adopted to greater or lesser extents. Other well known names whose layouts hail from that period include Derek Naylor with the *Aire Valley Railway*; David Mander with *Stronalachar*; Ted Polet and the *Craigcorrie and Dunalistair*; and David Burleigh with his *Llanmynach & Tawel-Llety*: the latter two layouts still see regular use to this day.

We should also, at this point, record the *Roth Valley Railway* which was established by Paul Windle in the late 1960s. That too was in the ilk of Hancock, but Paul's original version, which he built around the walls of his bedroom – now long gone and never photographed – had to be resurrected, not as a complete layout, but as numerous separate layouts, each depicting sections of his original network. Most notable is the *Crumley and Little Wickhill* section (see RAILWAY MODELLER January 2009), built with the help of friends and fellow modellers from Hull Miniature Railway Society and still making occasional appearances at shows in the UK.

To get a flavour of these historically relevant complete system layouts we have included over the next few pages, a selection of views of them, along with numerous other examples, arranged loosely in chronological order and starting with David Mander's *Stronalachar* from the 1970s.

Above
P D Hancock himself, seen at Bo'ness in an undated photograph.
Photo: courtesy Malcolm Macleod

Left
Where it all began...? as some would argue, P D Hancock's original *Craig and Mertonford* layout from the 1950s. Part of it still survives in the custody of various people and organisations, the Edinburgh & Lothians Miniature Railway Society being one of them, caring for Dundreich station as seen here with *Colin* at the head of a train. *Colin* was built in the 1960s using an N gauge Arnold chassis.
Photo: Malcolm Macleod

Right
The *Craig and Mertonford* seen in operation in the 1960s – although only the standard gauge section, and the tramway, can be seen in this view of the harbour area. The narrow gauge tracks were behind and to the left of the photographer!

Below
A scene on David Burleigh's *Llanmynach & Tawel-Llety Railway*, which he began in the spirit of P D Hancock 40 years ago in 1975. David is still building stock and running trains to this day.
Photo: Tim Easter

Stronalachar

By David Mander, in OO9

Layout information in brief

The Stronalachar Saga ran in a few early 1970s issues of RAILWAY MODELLER, describing the railway which was housed in a 21' x 12' room. The principal Station, Stronalachar itself, featured an interchange with the standard gauge feeder branch. The layout incorporated two complete circuits of the room, passing over some impressive crossings of waterfalls and rivers. The railway served several hamlets and industries along the way, in the manner of the real thing, and ended at a trans-shipment point at Port Banrich.

Aire Valley Railway

By Derek Naylor in OOn3

Layout information in brief

The original Aire Valley Railway was an exhibition layout, but some 50 years ago Derek rebuilt it into the loft at home. The principal station in the valley was Moorhead, and the railway interchanged with a harbour at Saltaire, where was located the locomotive facilities. The main line carried on up the valley to terminate at Nethertarn, whilst a branch left the main line at Moorhead to run to Stony Bridge.

Craigcorrie & Dunalistair

By Ted Polet in OO9

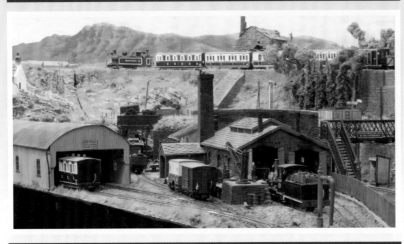

Layout information in brief

Perhaps the most notable modern take on a layout in the P D Hancock mould is the Craigcorrie & Dunalistair Railway, set too in Scotland but by the hand of Dutchman Ted Polet. From the harbourside at Craigcorrie, the line works its way up into the hills to the summit at Inverlochan, with Rae Bridge as the main intermediate calling point. From here an extension leads into another room in his house; the main layout measures 5'9" x 9'.

Gairloch & Wester Ross

By Roger Christian & Stan Williams in OO9

Layout information in brief

This L-shaped layout, built by two prolific builders of narrow gauge layouts, incorporates a spiral into its continuous run, all accommodated in a space measuring 8' x 7'. As the title suggests, this layout too is set in Scotland, but is operated by mostly colonial locomotive designs.

Subsequent to the layout's appearance in RAILWAY MODELLER in 2005, it was extended to the harbourside terminus and interchange called Loch Ewe, which was designed to be a standalone exhibition layout in its own right.

Spirals are a popular feature of narrow gauge layouts; in addition to the G&WR, Dick Wyatt installed one on his Dovey Valley Railway back in the 1970s, and of course the Ffestiniog Railway had to add a real one at Dduallt.

Roth Valley Tramway

By Paul Windle in OO9

1

2

3

Layout information in brief

Designed and constructed originally by Paul Windle, the Roth Valley Tramway has been the background to several successful OO9 layouts, built by him and fellow members of the Hull Miniature Railway Society. Most have been modest-size affairs, intended to showcase Paul's talents as a locomotive builder. They have included some kind of auxiliary working feature, such as the lifts and hoists on Moorton Bottom Yard. *One RVT layout, however, is anything but modest-sized; see overleaf...*

Photographs:
1. The prospective passenger's view of a train at Rothby station, high up the valley.
2. A Hunslet 0-4-2T arrives at the ultimate terminus of the line, Rothampton.
3. *Moorton Bottom Yard* was a small-space layout featuring a canal interchange.
4. Also on *Moorton Bottom Yard*, crates are loaded and unloaded magnetically.
5. A Hunslet crosses the road on the approach to Rothby station.
6. The branch to High Stamley featured Faller system working road vehicles.

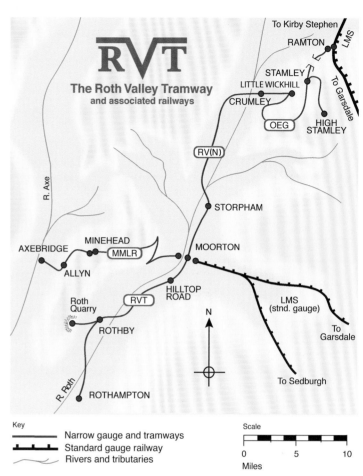

RVT

The Roth Valley Tramway
and associated railways

Narrow gauge railways and tramways of the Roth Valley

RVT   Roth Valley Tramway
MMLR   Moorton and Minehaed Light Railway
RV(N)   Roth Valley Northern
OEG   Overland Extension Group

Key

———— Narrow gauge and tramways
—■—■— Standard gauge railway
〜〜〜 Rivers and tributaries

Scale

0   5   10
Miles

Layout information in brief

Crumley & Little Wickhill *was the tour de force of the RVT saga: to replicate the sight of a real railway running up the side of a valley and turning back on itself required an unconventional shape and viewing angle in its 12' x 12' overall footprint. Nicknamed 'The Stealth Bomber' because of its shape, it is nevertheless a breathtaking piece of modelling – narrow gauge or not.*

Photographs:

7. A railcar in Crumley station; its stablemate high on the valley side is some 5' away.
8. The lonely outpost of Little Wickhill, where trains reverse to continue their run up or down the valley.
9. Working road vehicles using the Faller system also feature on this layout.
10. The opposing view to photograph 7, as a diesel-hauled goods train descends to Little Wickhill.

Ashbourne

Created in O-16.5

Layout information in brief

Ashbourne (Park Road) *was constructed by members of the Trent Valley Group of the 7mm Narrow Gauge Association, and represents a common carrier in its prime serving quarries in the Peak District.*

The layout is very flexible in its design, being essentially a modular layout which can be laid out in a variety of ways to suit exhibition requirements. The core layout is 22' x 6' to which extra sections can be added, giving a maximum overall size of 30' x 10'. Making a layout such as this in modules means that group members can build a small section in the comfort of their own home – even if they do not have space for a full layout – and enjoy operating their part of the whole layout during club nights or at exhibitions.

For more about the 7mm Narrow Gauge Association, see page 48.

Just supposing...

Earlier, in Chapter 1 we mentioned that the freelance approach to railway modelling is very popular, releasing the modeller from the restrictions that modelling an actual prototype incurs. We have just reviewed a selection of full system layouts created over the years, and as fine and exciting they are, not everyone has the space in which to build a full railway empire from one end to the other.

Devising smaller might-have-been layouts that feature just one narrow gauge station or freight installation is the next best way of realising the joy and fulfilment that narrow gauge modelling can bring, and countless other modellers have been doing that in all the various scale and gauge combinations. OO9 has been by far the most popular, with 7mm narrow gauge a close second, and other less adopted scale and gauge ratios following closely. All types of settings have been portrayed, from the quaint and rustic to the industrial and rusty!

Some of the most imaginative layouts have been those which just depict an industrial setting. *Barrowfleet*, built by members of Hull Miniature Railway Society 25 years ago, depicted the clay pits and brickworks of North Lincolnshire in the 1970s. To add extra operating interest, a section of the clay pit lines was developed as a 'heritage' section being run by a band of local enthusiasts, and, as it is set in North Lincolnshire, a short stretch of the British Rail branch to Barton-upon-Humber was included along the back. *Barrowfleet* has stood the test of time and can still occasionally be seen at exhibitions. Other more recent

Top
Disused clay pit workings in North Lincolnshire, represented by *Barrowfleet* by members of the Hull Miniature Railway Society. A train of empty skips passes the newly-created lake.

Right
Tate's Railway by Graham Morfoot, recreating the Lincolnshire potato railways of yore in a layout only 6' x 1'8". The standard gauge fiddle yard can be seen on the left. *Photo: Paul Bason*

layouts portraying industrial narrow gauge include Graham Morfoot's *Tate's Railway*, based on the former Lincolnshire potato railways; David Atkinson recreated the workings at a run-down lead mine in County Durham – *California Levels* – and James Hilton portrayed an aspect of ball clay mining in the Isle of Purbeck.

You see, Welsh slate isn't the only commodity to travel by narrow gauge railway!

The next leg of our own narrow gauge adventure takes a look at a small selection of the many and varied just supposing narrow gauge lines that have entertained countless visitors at shows up and down the country. We begin overleaf with an unusual Welsh narrow gauge line with a real historical basis but which was never built.

Right
David Atkinson built *California Levels* to 6mm to the foot scale: by using 9mm gauge trackwork this scaled out at exactly 18" gauge, whereas the more commonly found O9 – 7mm scale on 9mm track – is less precise. The layout represents a declining industry.
Photo: David Atkinson

Right
The peaceful surroundings of the Isle of Purbeck today belie the fact that once it was the scene of much industry, mining the ball clay prominent hereabouts. James Hilton built *Creech Bottom* in OO9 as a means of showcasing his collection of locos and stock.
Photo: James Hilton

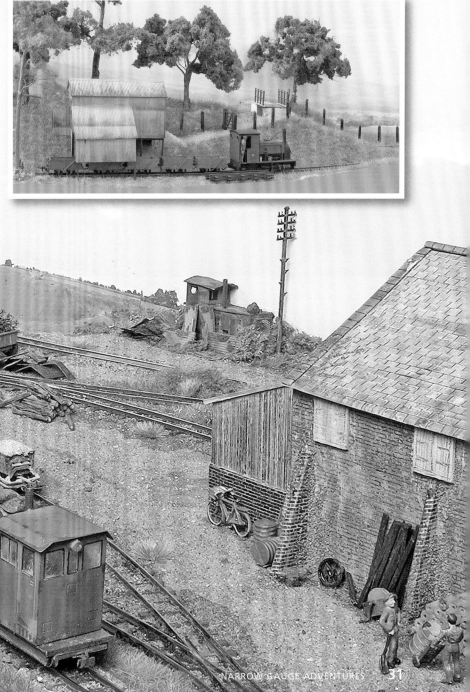

Beddgelert 1910

By Angus Watkins in OO9

Layout information in brief

Electrified narrow gauge railways are quite common in mainland Europe – especially Switzerland – but they have been comparatively rare in the UK. One project in the early 20th Century was the Portmadoc, Beddgelert & South Snowdon Railway, which was started but never completed.

Angus Watkins' layout takes the form of an automated diorama, and is the result of his wondering what the stillborn railway might have been like if it had been finished – the year 1910 being two years after that in which work stopped on the real thing.

Beddgelert 1910 boasts scratchbuilt locos, built with the aid of drawings of the prototypes, which were designed by Ganz of Budapest, Hungary. Coaches were built from Parkside kits and Worsley Works frets.

Bottle Kiln Lane

By John Thorne in OO9

Layout information in brief

Keen to model something set away from Welsh narrow gauge railways, John Thorne set the theme for his layout as a system serving a small pottery and interchanging with a canal basin.

Rather than running 'signature' narrow gauge locomotives such as Garratts – which would look out of place on a layout measuring only 6' x 2' in any case – Bottle Kiln Lane has a loco fleet of relatively small, common designs and a wagon stock of similarly small types.

A seasoned exhibitor, John intended Bottle Kiln Lane to be a project he could set up at home and work on. In common with Ashbourne (see page 28), it has modular sections which can be added, so Bottle Kiln Lane can be deployed either as a 6' long terminus or an 8' continuous run layout.

Bridport Town

By David Taylor in O-16.5

Layout information in brief

David Taylor has been building his own 'might have been' railway for many years: the Marshwood Vale links the Dorset coastal village of Charmouth with the town of Bridport, where interchange is made with the Great Western Railway. Built to 7mm scale, with hand-laid 16.5mm gauge track, it features scratchbuilt or kitbuilt locomotives and stock, and a superb selection of structures.

Bridport Town has an unusual design in that it is L-shaped, with only part of the GWR station and interchange modelled, along the shorter leg of this 9'4" x 7' layout.

The Pipe Yard

By David Lenton in O-16.5

Layout information in brief

David was inspired to build The Pipe Yard *by the large swathe of Staffordshire that was given over to kilns following the industrial revolution, firstly for making bricks, then pipes for the then modern sewers and suchlike. The plentiful supplies of coal and clay nearby meant these industries could be successful very quickly.*

The kilns themselves were made using a mix of card and styrene, and weathered heavily to recreate the appearance of these intensively-used buildings. To enhance things further, smoke units have been installed in the chimneys.

Balnakiel

By Ian Roberts in 1:22 scale (Gn15)

Layout information in brief

Balnakiel *represents a modern take on the traditional estate railway concept, as espoused by Sir Arthur Heywood amongst others. The idea behind the layout is that a railway continues to support the upkeep of the estate, bring in supplies and produce, and perhaps allowing some of the owning family a chance for a ride when possible!*

The layout is also to the relatively unconventional scale of Gn15, where 16.5mm gauge track is used to represent the Heywood 'minimum gauge' of 15" in 1:22, or G scale. Thus the range of items found in this popular outdoor scale can be used with reliable OO mechanisms.

Fakeham Tiles

By David Woodcock in O-12

Layout information in brief

David rose to a micro layout challenge for the EuroMOMING section of the October 2013 RAMMA exhibition in Sedan. In 7mm scale, the display size had to be equal to three A4 sheets, the track gauge less than 14mm, and there had to be at least one point. With 14mm ruled out, 9mm, 10.5mm or 12mm were the obvious possibilities; he decided on the last. Usefully, one of his O-14 locos and some Hudson tipper wagons could be re-gauged, while KBscale offered an O-12 version of one of its O14 loco kits.

Experimentation emphasised how small a space (just 127' x 30' in reality) the allowed size represented. The optimum track layout quickly evolved into a simple Y-shape with the two arms leading to off-stage loading and unloading facilities; gradients were added to maximise interest. David found prototype inspiration in the erstwhile line at Thakeham Tiles, not far from Brighton, where sand was conveyed from a loading facility in a former sand-pit down to a works complex.

Track was handbuilt using code 55 FB rail soldered to 4mm scale copper-clad sleepers, which provided an excellent representation of typical industrial narrow gauge track.

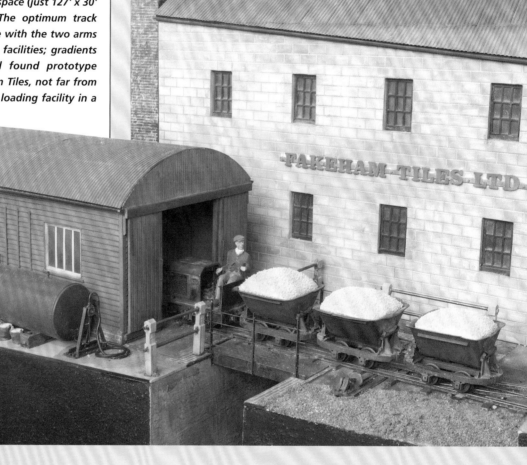

Modelling real prototypes

In the next chapter, on page 54, we look at many of the prototype lines in the British Isles including Ireland, which have fired the imagination of many a narrow gauge modeller and spawned hundreds of fictitious layouts, as we have seen on the previous pages. Not everyone likes to create a fictional railway though, choosing instead the more disciplined approach of building accurate models of prototype narrow gauge railway stations and lines. So, for the final leg of our narrow gauge journey of discovery we shall explore the work of modellers such as Peter Kazer,

Tim Tincknell, Rod Allcock and Paul Titmuss, who, amongst many others, settled for prototype railway locations as far afield as East Anglia, Ireland and the Isle of Man.

Such layouts are invariably of long-gone historical lines, so the challenges of modelling them can be quite tough, as archive material and photographs can be really difficult to unearth. There is however a surprising number of prototype narrow gauge railways in the British Isles from which to choose, and it's definitely not all in the Welsh tourist railway style.

The Lynton & Barnstaple Railway is probably the most widely recognised as a traditional railway system, being a passenger and goods-carrying concern and one which, until recently, was lost completely. It closed too soon for the notion of preservation to determine its fate.

In some ways the fact that it didn't survive is probably the reason why it is exalted so highly by enthusiasts and considered to be the benchmark by which many other narrow gauge layouts are based. We have already mentioned some of the other passenger carrying systems, such as the Leek & Manifold, the Ashover etc., that have given modellers completely fresh challenges and enabled the creation of distinctive models. One such modeller is

Left
The Southwold Railway was one of the handful of English 3' gauge railways, and rarer still in being a common carrier. Peter Kazer built this model in ¼" scale.

Below left
Alan Catlow recreated the old Manx Northern Railway station and surroundings of Ramsey in OOn3.

Below
Two views of another take on the Isle of Purbeck clay railways, *Pike's Pits*, this time modelled in 12mm scale by Peter Hollins. No two of the distinctive side- and end-tipping wagons were alike!

Above
A scene on the privately owned Statfold Barn Railway.
Photo: Graham Lightfoot

Peter Kazer, who began by building aspects of historical Welsh narrow gauge lines, then branched out, if you pardon the pun, to tackle subjects as diverse as the original 3' gauge Ravenglass & Eskdale, the Southwold Railway and the Sand Hutton estate railway. He works to an exceptional degree of accuracy and detail and has produced some of the finest narrow gauge models the hobby has ever seen. Accordingly we have included over the next few pages an example of his work to demonstrate further the delights that narrow gauge modelling can engender. In addition, of the many modellers who have also been driven to recreate miniature versions of British narrow gauge lines, we have taken a selection from across the spectrum, and in various scales and gauges, and present them as additional proof that there really is a lot to interest and inspire railway modelling beyond standard gauge.

So, as we said earlier, there will be something for everyone… And if all that isn't enough to ignite your thought processes, there are even modern-day incarnations of narrow gauge lines built by groups of enthusiasts on old standard gauge trackbeds, and proprietorial collections such as that of the former Abbey Light Railway from Kirkstall in Leeds (see page 47), and the latter day Statfold Barn collection (above), which can be great sources of inspiration too. Indeed the *Cressington Light Railway* built by Peter Leadley, was one such layout developed as a modern-day narrow gauge tourist line, albeit a 'just supposing' one, but proving that there are countless sources of ideas for the aspiring narrow gauge modeller.

Right
The *Cressington Light Railway*, by Peter Leadley, is an OO9 depiction of a supposed modern-day narrow gauge tourist railway.

Abergynolwyn

By Tim Tincknell in 5.5mm scale

Layout information in brief

Tim chose the unconventional scale of 5.5mm to the foot, utilising 12mm gauge track and mechanisms. This combination came about with the advent of TT in the late 1950s, but is still supported by a society today. Victorian locos, with their open cabs, would have visible motors in OO9, and 7mm scale would result in a layout being too big for its operational scope. Some FR body kits were produced by GEM for use with Tri-ang chassis, but these locos, representative of the Talyllyn Railway's early years, were modified from kits.

Corris

By Rod Allcock in OO9

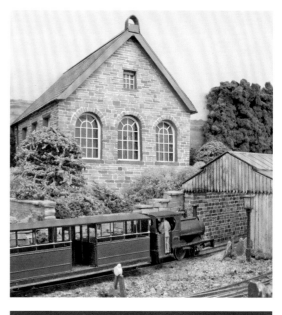

Layout information in brief

Thanks to a dedicated band of preservationists, efforts are being made to revive the Corris Railway; Rod set his model circa 1930, not long before passenger service ceased. The coaches were made from Worsley Works 'scratch aid' etches – that the stock is unoccupied tells its own story about how parlous things were for the railway at this time.

Corris has just the two locomotives, Nos.3 and 4, which were built from Rodney Stenning kits on scratchbuilt chassis with Mashima motors.

Sand Hutton

By Peter Kazer in 1:48 scale

Layout information in brief

The model depicts the hub of the railway at Sand Hutton (a village approximately 10 miles northeast of York) showing the workshops, station building and bridge across the River Stank. It is modelled to ¼" to 1' (1:48FS). Its stock and trackwork presented new challenges in this scale, and perhaps, remarks Peter, it might have been better to go up in scale!

The railway served a large agricultural estate, which Sir Robert Milo Walker inherited in 1920. Built to 18" gauge, the railway was all but gone by 1935.

3

4

Photographs:
1. The track climbs past the shed to cross the Stank on the simple and unprotected bridge, the piers of which survive.
2. A typical train crosses the Stank with five wagons. The river was made with polyester resin poured in layers on a gravel bed.
3. Two locomotives sit outside the workshop which also served as the running shed. The strange end window is clearly visible as is the unusual clerestory roof.
4. An approaching train, seen from the station crossing. The fencing around the station was typical estate post and rod, most of which disappeared for scrap after the railway closed.

Annascaul

By Paul Titmuss in OOn3

Layout information in brief

Annascaul was a crossing place on the storied 3' gauge Tralee & Dingle Railway, which linked the two towns of its title in south-west Ireland. It lingered on until June 1953, most famously with the monthly cattle specials which frequently were double-headed.

Paul's layout occupies a space of 16'6" x 1'6" over its scenic section, with fiddle yard boards at either end.

Abbey Light Railway

By David Malton in O-14

Layout information in brief

The Abbey Light Railway was a 2' gauge line that ran along a patch of wooded parkland near the ruins of Kirkstall Abbey in the middle of suburban Leeds. Construction started in 1978 by Peter Lowe, who was a lecturer at Leeds Technical College, helped by his family and a group of enthusiastic friends, including David's Dad from the beginning and himself when he was old enough join him. After Peter died, it closed in 2012.

O-14 was a new one to David; he chose it upon realising that there are kits available for some of the ALR loco types. Kirkstall Abbey station, or 'The Abbey End' as it was known, was chosen as its simple track plan was not too daunting as a starter to hand-building track.

The 7mm Narrow Gauge Association

An Introduction by long term Association member Peter Page

Castell Caernarfon, built and photographed by Keith Millard in 7mm/ft scale, built from Worsley Works etches and powered by 'Black Beetle' motor units

The Association was founded in 1979 to encourage, support and promote the modelling of narrow gauge railways in scales around 7mm/ft. It achieves this in many ways but a major benefit of membership has always been the magazine *Narrow Lines*, which is issued to members six times a year. *Narrow Lines* is now produced in full colour with a contents mix typical of model railway magazines and usually including material about the prototype to provide inspiration. Information about the Association's activities and related events is contained in the separate *Narrow News* which accompanies each issue of *Narrow Lines*. The Association also produces more focused publications including two which will be of particular help to newcomers – *Getting Started in 7mm Narrow Gauge* and the *Small Layouts Handbook*, a collection of layout examples with track plans.

One of the best pieces of advice that I was given when I first started modelling the narrow gauge in O-16.5 was to join the 7mm Narrow Gauge Association. It is over 20 years since I decided to follow that advice and I've never regretted doing so. The Association caters for all who model narrow gauge railways in and around the O gauge group of scales. This includes British O gauge (7mm/ft – 1:43.5), European 1:45 scale O gauge, and the American O gauge scale of ¼"/ft (1:48). Members use a variety of track gauges, currently from 6.5mm (to represent miniature railways with gauges between 10" and 12") to 24.5mm (representing 3'6" gauge). Although the majority work in British O-16.5 or American On30 using 16.5mm gauge track, there are sizeable minorities using 9mm or 14mm gauge.

The Association is UK based but our membership and our inspiration is global. We are a very tolerant organisation welcoming equally novices who are happy to create freelance locomotives using inexpensive OO ready-to-run models and a few pieces of plasticard, experts who scratchbuild specific prototypes in metal incorporating every bit of known detail, and all those in between. The one thing we don't do is to lay down modelling standards.

We encourage the formation of Area Groups in parts of the country where there are enough members to make regular meetings viable. Each Group is different but most meet monthly. Many Groups organise open events each year designed to attract interested modellers from a wider area than their usual catchment. The Association's own public exhibition is held annually in connection with the AGM, traditionally in the English East Midlands. All these meetings and events provide an opportunity for the scattered community of narrow gauge railway modellers working in the O gauge scales to share information and experiences face to face. Talking is a key activity.

Narrow gauge railway modelling in the O gauge scales is a specialist market. To fill gaps left by the trade the Association has two sales operations in addition to its publications work. Modelling Goods Sales provides a range of items that might otherwise be hard to get, including a few Association exclusives. Secondhand Sales provides a route for re-homing models that become surplus to their original owner's requirements. If you want to get a feel for this type of modelling before making any large commitments a few 'cheap and cheerful' purchases from Secondhand Sales may be the way to go.

Reading this, you're probably interested in modelling the narrow gauge, a field of railway modelling with an enormous range of prototype inspiration. A lot of the enjoyment and reward in that field comes from creating your own models. If you choose to do that in one of the O gauge scales, big enough to see but small enough to fit into any home, then the 7mm Narrow Gauge Association is for you.

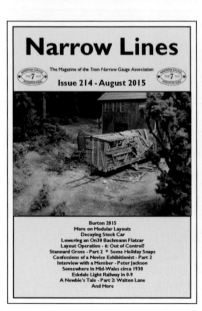

0-9 by Neil Smith

0-16.5 by Peter Jackson

On30 by Colin Hayes

Photographs courtesy Neil Smith, Peter Jackson and Richard Coney

Narrow gauge modelling in the O gauge group of scales – big enough to see but small enough to fit into any home

MILLIE STREET KIRKCALDY
FIFE SCOTLAND
KY1 2NL
Telephone and fax: 01592 640896
Website: www.dundasmodels.co.uk
Email: sales@dundasmodels.co.uk

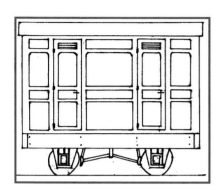

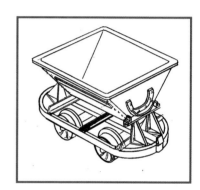

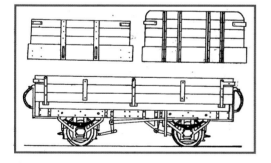

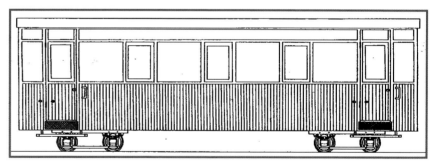

009 & 00n3 KITS

Freelance Panelled 4-Wheel 3rd Class 2 Compartment Coach……………….……….……...…...…….Ref.   DM75
Vale of Rheidol 3rd Class Bogie Coach Nos. 1-12……………………………..………………........Ref   DM10A
W.W.1 War Dept. Class D Dropside Bogie Open Wagon…………………..………………..………...Ref.   DM18
Hudson "V" Tipper Wagon…………………………………………………...……………………….Ref.   DM37
Welsh Highland Railway "Bro Madog Eisteddfod" Bogie Coach…...………………….……………..Ref.   DM40
Irish N G Open Goods Wagon………………………………………..………………………….......Ref.   DM77

The products illustrated above are just a selection of the wide range of narrow gauge rolling stock kits we produce for 4mm Scale Narrow Gauge Modellers. Festiniog, Festiniog & Blaneau, Freelance, Glyn Valley , Robert Hudson, Lynton & Barnstaple, Snailbeach District Railways, Tralee & Dingle, Vale of Rheidol, Welsh Highland Railway & W.W.1 War Department are all covered. We also produce loco kits to complement our rolling stock kits.

As the leading UK 4mm Scale Narrow Gauge Specialists our aim to provide the narrow gauge modeller with the widest selection of products available. We therefore stock the products of other manufacturers including kits, track & accessories, ready to run, locomotive chassis and narrow gauge books.

All these products can be found on our illustrated website and orders places via our online shop or direct to us by phone or fax or by post. Our illustrated catalogue is available (£2 includes £1 voucher against your first order).

LYNTON & BARNSTAPLE NARROW GAUGE '009'
Additional models added to the popular narrow gauge line

Image of 9951 courtesy of PECO

9951   SOUTHERN 760 'EXE'   SRP **£209,95**

9950   Lynton & Barnstaple 1361 'YEO'   SRP **£209,95**

9952   SOUTHERN 761 'TAW'   SRP **£209,95**

9953   SOUTHERN 760 'EXE'   SRP **£209,95**

9954   SOUTHERN 759 'YEO'   SRP **£209,95**

9955   Lynton & Barnstaple 1362 'EXE'   SRP **£209,95**

9956   Lynton & Barnstaple 1363 'TAW'   SRP **£209,95**

NEW!

Re-tooled model for the following projected releases;

9960 -   E188 'LEW' in Southern lined green *(original)*
9961 -   190 'LYD' in plain black livery
9962 -   30190 'LYD' in lined BR black
9963 -   E190 'LYD' in SOUTHERN lined green
      (Loco 190 is the 'new-build' prototype)

Subject to misprints and price changes. Please note that colours shown are for illustration purposes only

www.heljan.dk   UK contact - heljanuk@yahoo.co.uk   f VISIT US AT FACEBOOK.COM/HELJANAS   HELJAN

Chapter 3

British narrow gauge railways

The early part of the 20th century was arguably the heyday of narrow gauge railways in the British Isles, with numerous locomotive-worked systems spread across England, Wales, Scotland and Ireland. The majority served industrial needs, such as the transporting of slate from mines in North Wales (most were originally horse-drawn), but there were also many that were primarily passenger carriers including, famously, the Lynton & Barnstaple Railway in Devon and the steam and electric rail systems on the Isle of Man.

Narrow gauge systems in the British Isles covered a vast array of gauges and standards – from 18" to 4' – but most were small, self-contained operations so there was no need for any standardisation or compatibility between them. A nominal gauge of 1'11½" (usually referred to as a round 2') was popular for lines in North Wales, the small gauge having a number of advantages when laid over and through the rough and rugged terrain that was a hallmark of that part of the British Isles; these included the use of sharper curves, whilst the consequently smaller loading gauge equated to a reduction of the construction costs for tunnels, bridges, locomotives and rolling stock.

Whilst the industrial narrow gauge systems tended to be lightly laid – often quite ramshackle – affairs, in contrast

Below
The Corris Railway was one of three Welsh narrow gauge lines that eventually came under Great Western Railway ownership. Kerr Stuart 0-4-2ST No.4 leaves Machynlleth with a short rake of empty slate wagons, bound for Corris.
Photo: Rail Archive Stephenson

Right
The 2'3" gauge Campbeltown & Machrihanish Light Railway was the only public passenger carrying narrow gauge line in Scotland. Seen here is the harbourside terminus at Hall Street, Campbeltown, which linked with Clyde paddle steamer services. One of the railway's two Barclay 0-6-2T locomotives, *Atlantic*, is seen at the head of a passenger working on 2 August 1930.
Photo: H C Casserley

Below
The 3' Southwold Railway, which opened in 1879, linked Southwold and the sea with Halesworth. It followed the course of the River Blyth and had three intermediate stations. The railway closed in 1929. Here Sharp Stewart 2-4-0T No.3 *Blyth* is pictured (c.1912) at the extensive Southwold terminus.
Photo: Rail Archive Stephenson

the passenger carrying lines (particularly those eventually owned and operated by one of the Big Four railway companies) were of much more substantial construction with the use of a heavier gauge of rail section, together with greater investment in locomotives, rolling stock and infrastructure – including, in some cases, full signalling. However, lines that were built under the terms of the Light Railways Act of 1896 allowed a relaxation of certain requirements, such as level crossing gates, but with restrictions on line speeds of no more than 25mph.

Of the countries that make up the British Isles, Wales and Ireland held the greater concentrations of narrow gauge systems. Scotland, on the other hand, had very few lines – despite its size – with the Campbeltown and Machrihanish Light Railway being the county's only public passenger carrying narrow gauge line. The six mile 2'3"

gauge railway carried coal from local collieries (and passengers from 1906).

Jersey also boasted narrow gauge lines, both a 3'6" gauge passenger carrying railway that eventually ran for 8½ miles but closed in 1936, and mineral-only operations that served quarries on the island. Following the German occupation of the Channel Islands in WW2, German forces rebuilt the former passenger carrying line to metre gauge, motive power taking the form of tank engines requisitioned from Germany and France. It was dismantled after the occupation.

The last significant public narrow gauge line to open in the British Isles was the Ashover Light Railway in 1924. However, even before this date the heyday of narrow gauge railways had passed, with notable railways closing

soon after including the Southwold Railway in 1929 and the Lynton & Barnstaple Railway six years later.

Most narrow gauge railways disappeared during the first half of the 20th century, but there are many examples that survive, or have been re-opened as preserved lines. The former slate-carrying line from Tywyn in North Wales – now the Talyllyn Railway – was in fact the world's first preserved railway, being re-opened by enthusiasts in 1951. Numerous narrow gauge heritage operations have been established since that pioneering venture, with some examples – such as the Bala Lake Railway and the 2' gauge Gartell Light Railway in Somerset – occupying the track beds of former standard gauge routes.

Aside from the heritage operations, there are a few narrow gauge systems in the British Isles that continue to operate for industrial and military purposes, a significant example being the Eastriggs munitions depot in Dumfries and Galloway. Narrow gauge railways can also be found at several tourist attractions around the UK, including the 2'6" gauge system at Whipsnade Zoo, which utilises stock from the former Bowaters Light Railway.

It is beyond the scope of this publication to provide any sort of definitive list or point of reference for all the narrow gauge railways in the British Isles, past and present. What follows is a selection of prototypes, which serves to illustrate many of the aforementioned points and to demonstrate the variety that exists for modellers to exploit. Narrow gauge systems each had their own quirks, charm and character which made them unique, which means from a modelling perspective there really is something to satisfy all tastes, it's just a case of knowing where to look!

Above
Snowdon Mountain Railway is Britain's only rack railway. This 1964 view shows SMR No.2 *Enid* heading towards the summit, having just passed a train in Clogwyn station loop, visible in the background.
Photo: Geoff Plumb

Below
The 2' gauge Leighton Buzzard Light Railway was constructed to carry sand from local quarries to the standard gauge line from Leighton Buzzard to Dunstable. Simplex No.7 heads a train of Hudson tipper wagons on 1 July 1967.
Photo: Geoff Plumb

Left
The 1'11½" gauge Ashover Light Railway opened as late as 1924. Here ALR Baldwin 4-6-0T *Hummy* waits to leave Clay Cross c.1935.
Photo: Rail Archive Stephenson

Talyllyn Railway

The pre-preservation Talyllyn Railway was unusual amongst the narrow gauge lines serving the slate industry in that it was owned by the only quarry it served, but also ran a public passenger and freight service.

Slate was first quarried at Bryn Eglwys in the 1840s and was at first transported to the coast at Aberdyfi by horse and cart for onward shipment. The quarry was developed in 1863 under new ownership, with construction of a railway from the quarry to Tywyn, where it could connect with the standard gauge network.

Engineered by James Swinton Spooner, the line was straightforward to build, with a ruling gradient of 1:60 and the viaduct at Dolgoch being the only significant engineering feature. Running from Tywyn to Abergynolwyn, it continued into the valley of the Nant Gwernol and reached the lower level of the quarry via two inclines.

The Talyllyn Railway Company was formed in 1865, with public passenger operation commencing in late 1866. However, an inspection by the Board of Trade prior to the start of passenger services resulted with the implementation of several changes; the limited clearances of overbridges necessitated the slewing of the formation and permanent locking of the carriage doors on one side.

The railway's only two steam locomotives comprised 1864-built 0-4-2ST (named *Talyllyn*, later TR No.1) and 1866-built 0-4-0 back/well tank (named *Dolgoch*, later TR No.2), both built by Fletcher Jennings & Co.

William McConnel bought the railway and quarry in 1881 and, following his death in 1902, they were taken over by his son. Following expiration of the lease on the land and closure of the quarry in 1909, the concern was bought by Henry Haydn Jones in 1911, forming the Abergynolwyn Slate & Slab Co. to operate the quarry, having negotiated a new lease with the landowners.

The quarry business declined steadily after WW1, finally closing after a serious collapse in 1946. Haydn Jones continued to operate the railway, albeit just a summer-only passenger service; years of underinvestment had left *Dolgoch* as the only servicable locomotive and the track in a very poor state of repair. Following the death of Haydn Jones in July 1950, his widow kept the railway operating until the end of that season.

Preservation

A group of enthusiasts, led by the engineer and author, Tom Rolt, formed the Talyllyn Railway Preservation Society and took over the railway from Lady Haydn in February 1951, starting what was the world's first preserved railway. On 14 May that year the TRPS ran its first trains, going as far as Rhydyronen, with services to Abergynolwyn starting the following month.

Ex-Corris Railway locomotives Nos.3 and 4 were purchased to provide relief for the extremely wear-worn *Dolgoch*. 1953 saw much work to improve the condition of the track and another locomotive arrived, becoming TR No.6. Additional rolling stock was sourced from the Penrhyn Quarry Railway.

The 1960s saw further development at Wharf station and Abergynolwyn, together with the installation of passing loops to increase line capacity. Both the original TR locomotives were rebuilt and returned to service.

The running line was extended from Abergynolwyn to a new terminus (named Nant Gwernol) built at the foot of the first of the former quarry inclines. A Light Railway Order was required, passenger trains having never previously traversed this section. The first trains ran to here in 1976.

The railway has continued to develop ever since. The motive power fleet was bolstered with the completion of TR 0-4-2T No.7 in 1991, effectively a new-build steam locomotive that was completed at the railway's Pendre Works using components from a former 3' gauge Irish narrow gauge locomotive. Wharf Station was subject to significant rebuilding in 2003/4. 2015 saw major celebrations as the TR celebrated 150 years since the railway was first built.

Above
An early preservation era view of Tywyn station (c.1960s) with TR No.1 *Talyllyn* preparing to depart with a passenger train. The standard gauge crane in the background is occupying the former interchange siding.
Photo: Ron Fisher

Below
TR No.7 *Tom Rolt* at Nant Gwernol on 14 May 2001.
Photo: Andrew Burnham

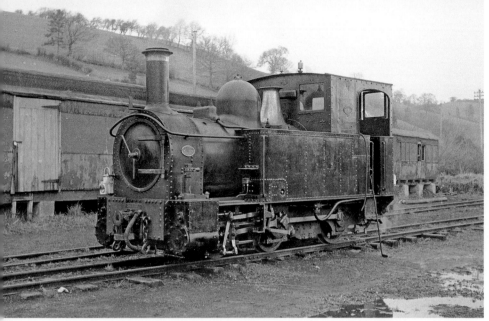

Welshpool & Llanfair

The 2'6" gauge line operated between Welshpool main line station to Llanfair Caereinion, with passenger services commencing on 4 April 1903. A feature of the line was in Welshpool itself where the line ran through the town, along the roadside and between buildings, to link with the standard gauge station. The line continually struggled to prove itself to be financially successful, aside from a brief increase in traffic during WW1.

The line (owned by the Cambrian Railways company) was absorbed by the Great Western Railway in 1923. Passenger traffic reduced further, ironically in part due to a bus service operated by the GWR, with services eventually ceasing during 1931. Freight traffic continued (under British Railways following nationalisation) until 3 November 1956. The line was preserved soon after and currently operates over most of the original route, between a terminus on the outskirts of Welshpool and Llanfair.

Original W&L Beyer-Peacock 0-6-0T locomotives (Cambrian Railways Nos.1 and 2) survive and continue to operate on the preserved railway. Built in 1902, they were renumbered as Nos.822 and 823 by the GWR and – following rebuilding in 1930 – received copper-capped chimneys and brass safety bonnets.

Above
Sporting a decidedly GWR appearance – note the copper-capped chimney and brass safety bonnet – No.822 is recorded at Llanfair on 22 April 1962.
Photo: Rail Photoprints

Above
A view from the cab of No.822 taken on 9 June 1956 on the approach to Raven Square at the start of the section through the streets of Welshpool.
Photo: Robert Darlaston.

Below
A busy scene at Llanfair in May 1956 with No.822 at the head of a mixed rake of wagons. Note the old standard gauge coach body on the right.
Photo: Colour Rail

Below
Looking south along the narrow gauge yard at Welshpool, with the standard gauge visible on the left. 17 November 1952.
Photo: Rail Photoprints

Vale of Rheidol

Below
Wearing BR corporate blue livery, No.7 departs Aberystwyth on 2 June 1971. A Class 24 can be seen in the adjacent platform.
Photo: Colour Rail

Below right
No.9 awaits departure from Devil's Bridge with an afternoon train (with coaches in BR crimson and cream livery) in August 1954.
Photo: Rail Photoprints

Opened in 1902, originally to carry both freight (lead ore and timber) and passenger traffic, the 1'11½" line linked with the standard gauge at Aberystwyth station. Climbing the 700ft to Devil's Bridge, there were three intermediate stations along the original 11¾ mile route, at Llanbadarn, Capel Bangor and Nantyronen.

Formerly operated by the Cambrian Railways company, the 1923 Grouping saw the line absorbed by the Great Western Railway. The new owner quickly withdrew the goods service and closed the branch that transported freight commodities to the harbour, deciding to concentrate purely on the passenger traffic which had increased as a result of tourists using the line to view the spectacular water falls at Devil's Bridge. Winter passenger services were withdrawn in 1930, and the line closed completely for the duration of WW2.

Ownership passed to British Railways following nationalisation in 1948, ultimately surviving to become the last steam railway owned by British Rail until its privatisation in 1989 (prior to which the stock, including steam locomotives, infamously sported BR rail blue livery with double-arrows).

The railway is now owned by a charitable trust, and continues to use the three 2-6-2T locomotives (Nos.7, 8 & 9) originally built for the line by the Great Western Railway between 1923 and 1924 at Swindon Works.

Ffestiniog Railway

The 1'11½" gauge Ffestiniog Railway was constructed between 1833 and 1836 to transport slate from quarries around Blaenau Ffestiniog to the coastal town of Porthmadog for loading onto ships. There was also later a connection with the standard gauge rail network at Minffordd. The line was down grade all the way to the coast, allowing loaded slate trains to run by gravity, with empty wagons hauled back up to the quarries by horse. The horses travelled down the line on 'dandy' wagons as part of the loaded consists, which also employed two brakesmen to control the speed of the train on the – almost continuous – 1:80 gradient by applying the brakes as required.

Steam traction arrived in 1863 in the form of *Mountaineer* and *Princess*, both 0-4-0STTs (saddle tank tender locomotives) constructed by George England & Co, six of this type eventually being built for use on the FR. The first of the railway's iconic 0-4-4-0T double Fairlie articulated locomotives arrived in 1869 named *Little Wonder*. Three further double fairlies followed, together with a single Fairlie 0-4-4T *Taliesin*.

The Festiniog Railway was the first narrow gauge railway to run public passenger services, approval being given officially in 1865, although it is known that passengers were carried – unofficially – as early as 1850. Passenger vehicles were originally small four-wheeled vehicles affectionately referred to as 'Bug Boxes', later augmented with bogie coaches from 1872. Vacuum braking was installed in 1893.

Although steam haulage took over from horses on up trains – with mixed formations comprising passenger vehicles, general goods vehicles and empty slate wagons – down slate trains continued to be worked by gravity.

Top left
One of the FR's iconic double Fairlie locomotives, 1879-built *Merddin Emrys*, shunts slate wagons at Porthmadog in May 2001. *Photo: Andrew Burnham*

Below left
Part of the now lost section of original FR route between Dduallt and Moelwyn Tunnel and on to Tanygrisiau station. This August 1966 view is looking towards the tunnel entrance from the Dduallt end.
Photo: Geoff Plumb

Below
A 2005 view of the joint station at Blaenau Ffestiniog, with 1979-built FR double Fairlie *Earl of Merioneth* running round its train as an Arriva Trains Wales Class 150 DMU prepares to depart for Llandudno.
Photo: Craig Tiley

Preservation

Following moves by enthusiasts to resurrect the railway as a tourist attraction, Alan Pegler purchased the railway company in 1954, clearing its debts and becoming the new company's first chairman.

The line was gradually re-opened for passenger services in stages, reaching Tan-y-Bwlch in 1958 and Dduallt in 1968. North of this point, however, the original formation had been lost following construction of the Ffestiniog hydro-electric power station and its reservoir (Llyn Ystradau). This required construction of a 2½ mile diversionary route, with a spiral at the southern end (unique on a public railway in the British Isles), together with a new 310-yard long tunnel. This huge task was completed over a period of 13 years, with the original route being rejoined at Tanygrisiau station, which was re-opened in 1978. Blaenau Ffestiniog – 13½ miles from Porthmadog – was reached in 1982, with a new joint station opened in collaboration with British Railways, built on the site of the original GWR station.

The connection with the restored WHR at Porthmadog was reinstated in 2011.

The preserved FR utilises much original rolling stock, together with original examples of the George England & Co 0-4-0STTs and the double Fairlies. Two new double Fairlies have been constructed by the preserved railway; *Earl of Merioneth* in 1979 and *David Lloyd George* in 1992. Single Fairlie *Taliesin* is technically a rebuild of the original locomotive (completed in 1999), it utilising components from the 1876-built locomotive, but was essentially built completely from scratch. Other notable FR stalwarts include the former Penrhyn Quarry Railway 2-4-0STT locomotives *Blanche* and *Linda*, which arrived on the railway in the 1960s.

Top
Former Penrhyn Quarry Hunslet 2-4-0STT *Linda*, runs off the Cob with a passenger service. In the background is Porthmadog. Behind the photographer are the locomotive shed and workshops at Boston Lodge.
Photo: Ron Fisher

Above
1864-built George England 0-4-0STT *Palmerston* at Porthmadog Harbour Station in 1934. The leading vehicle is one of the railway's original 'bug box' carriages.
Photo: Ffestiniog Railway Archive

Ownership of the FR changed in 1921, with the new chairman also holding the same position with the neighbouring Welsh Highland Railway. This led to joint management of the two companies, and connecting of the two railways at Porthmadog in 1923. Following a combination of declining slate traffic on both the FR and WHR, together with unrealised tourist traffic on the WHR, light railway operation was introduced on both in a bid to reduce running costs, with the prolific light railway engineer, Colonel H F Stephens appointed to assist with the implementation. However, the WHR continued to struggle and became bankrupt in 1933, it being leased thereafter by the FR to enable it to continue to operate. Following further losses the WHR closed to passenger traffic in 1936 and goods a year later.

1939 saw the cessation of passenger services on the FR, after which gravity operation of down slate trains also stopped. Slate traffic ended in 1946, but the railway and its infrastructure remained in place as a result of there being no provision in the original Act of Parliament for its closure.

Welsh Highland Railway

Aside from the slate quarry operations that were already well established in the vicinity of Snowdonia in North Wales, the late 19th century saw a further proliferation of narrow gauge lines in the area (including of course, the Snowdon Mountain Railway), prompted by the growth in tourism and the passenger traffic opportunities that this presented.

Several companies attempted to exploit this market, one such being the North Wales Narrow Gauge Railway, which had plans for several lines in the area, including the construction of a 1'11½" gauge line running from Dinas to Rhyd Ddu. Opened in sections from 1877, the planned extension to Beddgelert never materialised and passenger operations ceased on the route during WW1, with just freight traffic thereafter.

South of the NWNGR's route was a five mile section of line constructed from 1901 by the Portmadoc, Beddgelert & South Snowdon Railway. It reached Beddgelert but never connected with the NWNGR at Rhyd Ddu.

Construction of the line to connect Rhyd Ddu and Beddgelert, via the Aberglaslyn Pass, commenced in 1905 but following financial difficulties, it was never completed and the work, which included the tunnels in the Aberglaslyn Pass, was abandoned.

The Welsh Highland Railway (Light Railway) Co. was established in 1922 and, with the aid of goverment loans, modified and extended the existing lines. The line was opened throughout between Dinas and Portmadog in 1923. Later that year the two remaining original NWNGR locomotives (*Russell* and single Fairlie *Moel Tryfan*) were joined by Baldwin 4-6-0T No.590. The connection with the Ffestiniog Railway at Portmadog (and joint station), allowed the FR's George England locomotives and carriages to be used on the line, bolstering the rather sparse collection of WHR stock.

The WHR always struggled financially, it being effectively crippled by the loan repayments it owed. Passenger services became seasonal only as of 1924, with goods services running as required. Despite cost-cutting measures implemented by Colonel Stephens, and joint management of the WHR and FR (with the FR leasing the WHR), traffic on the WHR finally ceased in 1937.

Preservation

In the early 1960s enthusiasts formed a society which later became the Welsh Highland Light Railway (1964) Co., establishing a base at Porthmadog and running public services on a short length of line from 1980.

However, in the late 1980s it emerged that the FR had its own plans to re-open the WHR, starting at Caernarfon and working back to Porthmadog, connecting with the FR to create a 40 mile railway.

With the authorisation of a Light Railway Order for the Dinas – Caernarfon section (which traces the route of the former LNWR standard gauge line that closed in 1964), the FR started work in 1997, with services commencing along this stretch in October that year. The railway opened as far south as Rhyd Ddu in 2003.

The WHLR (1964) Co., by now registered as the Welsh Highland Railway Ltd, reached agreement with the FR to extend its own line northwards to Pont Croesor, and to run trains on this section until such time when it was reached by the FR.

The final phase of the WHR rebuilding, from Rhyd Ddu through Beddgelert and Aberglaslyn Pass to Porthmadog was completed in stages, reaching Pont Croesor in 2010.

The link at Porthmadog between the FR and WHR has since been re-instated, with the FR's Porthmadog station redeveloped to accommodate WHR trains.

WHR trains have been entrusted to former South African NGG16 Beyer Garratt locomotives, although FR locomotives have also frequently traversed the route. (However, the NGG16s exceed the loading gauge for working on the FR route to Blaenau Ffestiniog.)

Above
Welsh Highland Railway 2-6-2T *Russell*, built by Hunslet of Leeds in 1906, photographed in action on the original WHR. The locomotive was requisitioned for the war effort in 1941, working at an ironstone site in Oxfordshire. After the war it was sold to the Nordern Clay Mines in Dorset where it worked until 1953. Following preservation it returned to service in 1987.
Photo: Rail Archive Stephenson

Above left
A long way from its native South African stomping ground, 1958-built 2-6-2+2-6-2 NGG16 Beyer Garratt No.138 heads through the spectacular scenery of the Aberglaslyn Pass.
Photo: Andrew Burnham

Corris Railway

Corris, located on the border between Gwynedd and Powys in mid-Wales, was the location of the northern terminus of this 2'3" gauge line (originally a tramroad worked by gravity and horses) that was opened in 1859 and ran from Aberllefenni to Derwenlas, south east of Machynlleth. There were also branches that served numerous quarries *en route*, including the slate ones at Corris Uchaf and Aberllefenni.

The completion of a standard gauge route through Machynlleth in 1863 led to closure of the narrow gauge section between Machynlleth and Derwenlas, it being considered easier to convey slate direct to the standard gauge at Machynlleth. At the same time, an application was made to convert the tramroad to a railway, with the consequential upgrading for locomotive use.

Four locomotives operated on the Corris Railway; Nos.1 – 3 were 0-4-2STs constructed by Hughes Falcon Works in 1878 (all were originally built as 0-4-0STs), joined by Kerr Stuart 0-4-2ST No.4 in 1921.

Passenger services commenced in 1883; all platforms were on the east side of the line so the carriages and locomotives were equipped with doors on that side only. Slate traffic was always the main commodity transported on the railway, but timber was also carried between the first and second world wars and coal was carried for the local communities.

An unusual feature of the railway – for narrow gauge – was the overall roofs at its Corris and Machynlleth stations.

In 1930 the railway was sold to the Great Western Railway. The passenger service was withdrawn the following year. The line continued to operate slate traffic, surviving nationalisation in 1948 only to be closed soon after following serious erosion to the formation.

Preservation

Locomotives Nos.3 and 4, together with some of the original rolling stock, are preserved on the nearby Talyllyn Railway.

The Corris Railway Society was formed in 1966, it subsequently opening a museum on the site of the old engine shed at Maespoeth. In 2002 a short section of running line was opened to passengers and in 2005 the railway received its new-build steam locomotive (No.7), a replica of the original Kerr Stuart Corris locomotive.

Lynton & Barnstaple Railway

Running for a total distance of 19¼ miles in North Devon, the L&B, as it is usually referred to, opened as an independent railway in 1898, ostensibly as a passenger carrying line conveying tourists to the North Devon coast. Built to 1'11½" gauge and connecting the villages of Lynton and Lynmouth with the market town of Barnstaple, the line reached the standard gauge Ilfracombe branch at Barnstaple Town, with cross platform connections to branch trains and thence to London Waterloo.

The railway originally featured four intermediate stations, with three halts added later. The main engineering feature on the line was the impressive Chelfham viaduct.

The railway realised barely sufficient traffic revenue to remain viable. Competition from road transport during the early 1920s meant that it became uneconomic and, despite increased investment following its ownership passing to the Southern Railway, the line closed in late 1935.

A distinctive feature of the L&B was its locomotive fleet, which originally comprised a trio of Manning Wardle 2-6-2Ts named after local rivers; *Yeo*, *Exe* and *Taw*. *Lyn*, a Baldwin 2-4-2T was subsequently ordered to expand the motive power fleet, this being first used in 1898. A fourth 2-6-2T, *Lew*, was purchased in 1925, which featured various improvements to the original Manning Wardle design. Under Southern Railway ownership the locomotives latterly adopted the attractive Maunsell olive green livery, with black and white lining and 'Southern' lettering on the side tanks.

Coaching stock was both large and luxurious by narrow gauge standards, comprising 16 vehicles built by the Bristol Wagon & Carriage Works Co. Ltd, to six different types, and all measuring 39' 6" long by 6' wide and 8'7" high. An additional coach was added to the fleet in 1911, slightly longer than the others. Under L&B ownership, the vehicles were painted in an attractive maroon and cream livery,

with green livery being adopted under SR ownership.

The railway possessed an assorted collection of goods vehicles, although freight only workings were rare. The usual practice was to run mixed formations with the wagons attached to passenger trains.

Preservation

In 2004 a short section of line from Woody Bay station reopened to passengers, the original station buildings – purchased in 1995 – having survived *in situ* for 60 years. The line was extended to over a mile in 2006, running to a new temporary terminus at Killington Lane. At the time of writing there are plans to extend further south to the outskirts of Barnstaple. A replica of Baldwin 2-4-2T *Lyn* was completed at Alan Keef Ltd in autumn 2017 for use on the railway with the recently completed L&B bogie coaches (classed as rebuilds but effectively brand new), and parts exist for a replica of the Manning Wardle *Yeo*. A replica of one of the 2-6-2Ts has already operated on the preserved line, the Ffestiniog Railway having completed its new-build based on *Lyd* in 2010.

Above
The preserved station site at Woody Bay, which retains the original grand station buildings.
Photo: Ron Fisher

Below
L&BR 2-6-2Ts No E188 *Lew* and E761 *Taw* wait to leave Barnstaple with a mixed train in c.1926. The platform connected with standard gauge services on the other side and there was also an interchange siding for goods traffic situated behind the photographer.
Photo:
W H Whitworth/
Rail Archive Stephenson

Below right
A general view of Chirk
station on 14 August
1925 looking towards
Pontfaen, with the
standard gauge station
platform running along
the other side of the
fence (note the pagoda
waiting shelter). Visible
under the arch of the
narrow gauge bridge is
Sir Theodore, which is
running forward to
couple to the loaded
granite wagons in the
platform, before
propelling them up the
loading ramp for
transhipment to the
standard gauge.
*Photo: Rail Archive
Stephenson*

Below
Sir Theodore (built by
Beyer Peacock in 1888
and named after the
then chairman of the
GVT) awaits departure
from Glyn Ceiriog
station on 14 August
1925 with a passenger
train for Chirk.
*Photo: Rail Archive
Stephenson*

Glyn Valley Tramway

Running for 6½ miles along the picturesque Ceiriog Valley in north east Wales, the Glyn Valley Tramway was originally constructed to connect a slate quarry at Llansantffraid with the Shropshire Union Canal at Gledrid. Completed in 1872 for the conveyance of mineral and passenger traffic, the tramway was originally worked by horses and gravity.

Steam traction took over on the 2'4½" gauge line from 1888 and the line was re-routed at Pontfaen to provide an interchange with the GWR and the Shropshire Union Canal at Chirk. A two mile extension was also laid from Glyn to serve quarries around Pandy, with passenger services resuming in 1891 after being postponed for the rebuilding work.

The line was worked by three distinctive Beyer Peacock locomotives, which were distinguishable from conventional steam locomotive designs with their skirts that enclosed the wheels and motion – dictated by the Board of Trade regulations for tramway operation. These 0-4-2T locomotives were designed to run cab-forward, also to satisfy the tramway regulations which stipulated that the driver must be positioned at the front of the locomotive. The first two (named *Sir Theodore* and *Dennis*) were ordered in 1888, with the third, named *Glyn*, ordered in late 1891.

The trio was joined by a fourth locomotive in 1921, a Baldwin 4-6-0T which was rebuilt to suit the GVT by Beyer Peacock. Its design fell short of the Board of Trade regulations for tramway locomotives, but strangely this didn't prevent its use on the GVT.

Mineral traffic reduced from the late 1920s following competition from road transport, whilst a bus service in the valley introduced in 1932 saw a decline in passenger receipts.

The passenger service was reduced to one return trip in late 1932, ceasing completely in April the following year. Mineral traffic continued up to closure of the tramway in 1935. All the locomotives were scrapped in 1936, but two of the original carriage bodies survived and these are now preserved on the Talyllyn Railway.

Isle of Man

The rail network on the Isle of Man was developed in the late 19th century, built to narrow gauge standards to suit the terrain of the island. Unlike on the mainland where it was the transport of freight that most often initiated the construction of narrow gauge systems, here it was the embryonic tourism industry that prompted its development.

The first part of the 3' gauge Isle of Man railway opened in 1873, a 10 mile line connecting Douglas and Peel. Three new locomotives were ordered; 2-4-0Ts from Beyer Peacock. Passenger stock initially took the form of three-compartment four-wheel stock; the now familiar bogie stock was introduced from 1876. Rolling stock comprised – after 1926 – some 75 bogie and 14 six-wheel Cleminson coaches. The bodies from the original four-wheel coaches were retained, placed in pairs on a bogie chassis, with the four-wheel chassis converted into freight vehicles.

The line south from Douglas to Port Erin opened in 1874, with two more locomotives arriving to bolster the railway's motive power. The fleet of Beyer Peacock 2-4-0Ts eventually numbered 15, with the last arriving in 1926. The design was revised for the later examples but the whole class continued to retain a very similar external appearance. There was one other steam locomotive on the island; No.15 *Caledonia*, an 0-6-0ST that was built by Dübs, originally operating as No.4 on the Manx Northern Railway.

Two other steam railways were constructed on the island; the Manx Northern and the Foxdale Railway, both being subsequently absorbed by the Isle of Man Railway. (The 2½ mile section from St. Johns to Foxdale was built in 1886 to serve the lead mines in that area.) Two electrically powered railways were also constructed in the north eastern part of the island; the Manx Electric Railway and the Snaefell Mountain Railway, both opening in the 1890s.

The inter-war years proved to be the railway's heyday, with summer holiday traffic demanding trains of 14 or more coaches on the Douglas to Port Erin section. However, for winter services one-coach trains sufficed across the island.

Dedicated freight trains were not a regular sight, with wagons usually attached to passenger workings.

The railway suffered as a result of little maintenance through the years of WW2, and passenger figures declined thereafter – both as a result of a reduction in visitors to the island and also an increase in car ownership for residents. This led to reduced timetables and various cost-cutting measures, including the purchase of two railcars in 1961 from the closed County Donegal Joint Railways Committee. Services were suspended in November 1965 and, with the track in such poor condition, the railway remained closed throughout 1966.

In 1967, following the lease of the railway to Lord Ailsa, all the lines re-opened for summer traffic. However, with poor visitor numbers the following summer, the Ramsey and Peel lines closed in September 1968, leaving just the Douglas to Port Erin section (the last train on the Foxdale branch ran in 1957). The closed lines were lifted in 1974.

In 1972 the Isle of Man Railway Company resumed control with the help of government subsidies from the Manx tourist board. After a precarious few years, full line operations resumed between Douglas and Port Erin in 1977, with the railway company sold to the Manx government the following year. Numerous changes have been made in the intervening years, including the modernisation of platform infrastructure and level crossings.

The two electric railways continue to operate as heritage attractions, with the majority of the original routes and infrastructure surviving intact.

Leek & Manifold Railway

The Leek and Manifold Valley Light Railway was a 2'6" gauge line in Staffordshire that opened in 1904. The railway, which ran for 8¼ miles and followed the River Manifold for much of it, served as a feeder to the standard gauge network at Waterhouses (the end of the North Staffordshire Railway branch from Leek), carrying predominantly milk from dairies in the region. The most important traffic was from the Express Dairies Creamery in Ecton, with milk loaded directly into standard gauge tanker wagons, which were conveyed along the narrow gauge line on transporter wagons – the L&MLR being the first British narrow gauge railway to use such vehicles.

Also operating passenger services (there were eight intermediate stopping points), the railway was originally run by the NSR but after the Grouping in 1923 it came under the control of the London Midland & Scottish Railway.

Usually sufficing with just one engine in steam, the railway had just two steam locomotives; both were 2-6-4Ts built by Kitson & Co of Leeds, completed in 1904. Trains started at Hulme End, at the northern end of the line, where the engine shed was located.

The closure of the Ecton creamery in 1932 left the railway with insufficient freight traffic to continue as a viable operation. It closed completely in March 1934.

Below
Leek & Manifold Light Railway Kitson-built 2-6-2T No.2 *J B Earle* waits to leave Hulme End with a passenger train on 12 August 1933. The huge headlamps that adorned both of the L&MLR locomotives gave them a distinctly foreign appearance. In the background to the left are standard gauge coal wagons that have arrived on transporter wagons. To the right can be seen the railway's locomotive stabling area and servicing facilities.
Photo: Rail Archive Stephenson

Industrial systems

There was a time when most industrial operations in the British Isles featured a narrow gauge system of some sort, ranging from just a few yards of track to many miles, such systems suiting the often restricted spaces.

The large workshops of the London & North Western Railway and the Lancashire & Yorkshire Railway (at Crewe and Horwich respectively) both, famously, had internal narrow gauge systems.

The water industry made much use of narrow gauge systems, both at works complexes (Leeds and Harrogate for example), together with the construction of reservoirs, including the 3' gauge 22-mile line in Scotland that ran from Fort William to service the construction of a dam at Loch Treig.

Other significant applications included brick manufacturing and the paper industry in Kent (exemplified with the Bowater's Paper Mill Railway, below), together with numerous military sites. These include the extensive 18" network of the Royal Arsenal Railway, and the Eastriggs Munitions Depot, which was used to hold munitions for all three of the armed services.

Bowater's Paper Mill Railway

The Bowater's Paper Mill Railway was originally a horse drawn system, built in 1905 to serve the Sittingbourne paper mill in Kent, carrying the raw materials for the manufacturing of paper together with the finished product. Steam locomotives first arrived on the 2'6" gauge system in 1905 with a pair of Kerr Stuart Brazil class locomotives, named *Premier* and *Leader*.

Expansion of the mill at Sittingbourne was restricted so a new mill was built at Kemsley in 1923, which at the time was the largest paper mill in Europe. In its heyday, the railway system was a 24 hour a day, seven days a week operation, with a passenger service for mill employees. At its peak, the locomotive fleet numbered 16, comprising 12 steam, two fireless, one diesel and one battery electric.

The main running line was 3½ miles long and the system was made up of more than 10 miles of track in total. There was also an internal standard gauge line that connected with the national network via the Sheerness branch.

In 1965 a study of internal transport was made which concluded that this would be better achieved with road transport. Therefore in 1969 the railway was handed over to the Locomotive Club of Great Britain's Light Railway Section, which became the Sittingbourne & Kemsley Light Railway (SKLR).

Ownership of the mills changed several times following their sale by Bowater's in 1986. Production at the Sittingbourne mill stopped in 2007, prompting the end of operations on the railway. Subsequent negotiations with the owners led to the SKLR being given a 125 year lease for a mile of the railway. The Sittingbourne mill was demolished in 2010 but the mill at Kemsley (owned by a different company) continues to produces paper.

Left
In June 1961 Andrew Barclay 0-4-0WT *Cegin* hauls a rake of loaded slate wagons at Penrhyn Slate Quarry in North Wales.
Photo: Ron Fisher

Right
Quarry Hunslet 0-4-0ST *George B* (built-1898) emerges from a tunnel that connected two parts of the Dinorwic Slate Quarry at Llanberis in June 1961.
Photo: Ron Fisher

Far right
Empty slate wagons descend the rope worked Port Dinorwic incline which connected the port area to the terminus of the 4' gauge Padarn Railway (on which the slates were carried on transporter wagons).
Photo: Ron Fisher

Mineral lines

Narrow gauge systems were ideally suited to quarries and other mineral concerns, where raw materials from the ground (such as slate, coal, lead and clay) needed to be transported from the source of extraction to a transfer point for onward shipment, whether that be by water, rail or road. In most cases the extraction points moved over time, so the suitability of a narrow gauge setup lay in the ability to change or extend lines quickly and easily, thereby minimising any delays to operations.

The steel and ironstone industries were significant users of narrow gauge lines, with instances of the latter proliferating in Leicestershire and Northamptonshire (such as the Kettering Iron & Coal Co., which established a network of 3' gauge lines from the orefields to the furnaces at Kettering). Similarly, there were also former lead mines in Shropshire served by the Snailbeach District Railways, a short-lived 2'3¾" system.

Penrhyn

The slate industry in North Wales reached its zenith in the late 19th century, with this part of the British Isles becoming home to a huge number of quarrying operations, most with their own narrow gauge systems.

The 1'11½" system at Penrhyn was one of the most famous of these railways, which conveyed the slate from the quarries near Bethesda to the harbour at Port Penrhyn. First opened in 1801 and worked by horses, steam traction was adopted during the 1870s. A passenger service for quarrymen was operated until 1951. The declining slate traffic led to its closure in 1962, but two of the quarry's locomotives – *Blanche* and *Linda* – found new homes on the embryonic Festiniog Railway.

Dinorwic

This railway system linked the quarries near Llanberis with

Left
Finedon Ironstone Quarries in Northamptonshire operated a trio of Peckett-built 0-6-0STs on its 3'3" gauge system. No.87 (of 1942) is pictured here in September 1964, which had 12" cylinders in difference to 10" cylinders on the other two 1934-built machines. Visible either side of the locomotive are some of the railway's iron ore wagons, each underframe carrying a pair of five-ton skips. The railway closed in October 1966.
Photo: Ron Fisher

Photo: Ivo Peters

Below

The loading dock and transhipment shed at Furzebrook on the Isle of Purbeck, part of the 2'8" Furzebrook Railway. The narrow gauge line was at a higher level than the standard gauge to allow the contents of the narrow gauge wagons to be tipped directly into the standard gauge vehicles. Pictured here is *Tertius*, an 1886-built Manning Wardle 0-6-0ST. Its ungainly appearance was a result of being fitted with a second-hand boiler in 1951, sourced from one of the company's withdrawn locomotives, formerly used on its 3'9" gauge line at Norden. The firebox of this donor boiler was too wide to fit between the frames of *Tertius*, resultantly being perched on top.

Port Dinorwic, with a 1'10¾" line serving the quarry and a 4' gauge line (known as the Padarn Railway) used to convey the quarry trucks – on transporter wagons – from the quarry to the coast.

In its heyday the operation at the quarries was enormous, with over 2,000 wagons and 50 route miles of track.

The Padarn Railway also operated a passenger service for quarrymen until its closure in 1961, the remaining quarry railways closing in November 1967.

Many of the former quarry locomotives survive, whilst a section of the former Padarn Railway trackbed is now occupied by the 1'11½" gauge Llanberis Lake Railway. The former quarry workshops at Llanberis are now part of the Welsh Slate Museum.

South of England clay mines

There once existed a number of clay mines in the south of England, including the 4'6" Lee Moor Tramway that ran from quarries on the southwest slopes of Dartmoor to the coast at Plymouth – including the famous horse-worked

trains crossing the GWR main line at Laira – and the two systems in the Isle of Purbeck.

These comprised firstly the Furzebrook Railway, a 2'8½" gauge line operated by Pike Bros, Fayle & Co. to transport ball clay (an ingredient in the production of fine china) from its pits near Furzebrook and Creech to weathering beds and then onwards, initially to a wharf on the river Frome, but after WW2 to an interchange with the standard gauge Wareham to Swanage branch.

Secondly there was a 3'9" gauge line – operated by the same company – which connected a clay works at Norden with Poole Harbour, although this also was later cut back to connect with the Swanage branch, in this case at Norden. Relaid to 2' gauge in 1947, the line lasted until 1971. It utilised second-hand stock including the former Welsh Highland Railway locomotive, *Russell*.

The Purbeck Mineral & Mining Museum is dedicated to the local industrial operations in the area and is located adjacent to Norden station, near Corfe Castle, on the preserved Swanage Railway.

Irish railways

Ireland once boasted numerous 3' gauge narrow gauge railways, many of which were secondary passenger lines and all together totalled around 500 miles. The longevity of narrow gauge lines in Ireland – the closure of the last passenger carrying line was in 1961 – relative to those in England and Wales, can in part be attributed to the poor road networks and poverty within many rural communities, both serving to defer competition from road transport.

Despite the 3' gauge being a consistent feature of most Irish narrow gauge lines (there were no fewer than 18 at one time), the locomotives and rolling stock, however, varied considerably.

In Northern Ireland railways of note include the **Clogher Valley Railway**, which opened in 1887 (originally classified as a tramway) and ran for 37 miles – mostly alongside roads – from Maguiresbridge in County Fermanagh (where a station was shared with the Great Northern Railway of Ireland) through largely rural areas to Tynan in County Armagh, where it also connected again with the Irish standard gauge – 5'3" – network.

Steam traction held sway on the line for most of its existence, originally with a fleet of six 0-4-2Ts built by Sharp Stewart. These were joined by an 0-4-4T named *Blessingbourne* in 1910. In 1933 a 2-6-0T (from the defunct Castlederg & Victoria Bridge Tramway) was acquired from a scrap merchant in exchange for *Blessingbourne* and one of the life-expired 0-4-2Ts. It was rebuilt into a 2-6-2T, and painted maroon as CVR No.4, in which form it proved very successful.

The rural nature of the route always limited any potential traffic revenue that could be realised by the railway – it made a loss throughout most of its existence and relied on subsidies to keep it running. The GNR(I) was invited to

take over the railway, but it declined.

In the early 1930s diesel traction was introduced in a bid to reduce operating costs. Two vehicles, a railbus and rail lorry, were constructed by Walkers of Wigan. Ultimately, however, it was road competition and cost-saving measures during WW2 that spelt the end of the CVR, the last trains running on 31 December 1941.

The **Londonderry & Lough Swilly Railway**, which opened in 1883, is noteworthy; the rural nature of its route enabled the use of stock to a generous loading gauge, including eight-coupled locomotives that exhibited a bulk more akin to standard gauge counterparts; weighing over 50 tons, the railway's 4-8-4Ts were the heaviest narrow gauge tank locomotives used in the British Isles.

In the 1920s the railway company saw its future in road transport, migrating to freight only operations and bus services from 1929. Closure came in 1953.

The L&LSR was, in fact, one of two railways that crossed the border with the Republic of Ireland following the 1921 partition, which thereafter required customs formalities to be observed at border stations. (The other was the

Above
L&LSR 4-6-0T No. 3 is depicted here entering Tooban Junction and was one of four of this class delivered by Andrew Barclay to the Letterkenny and Burtonport Extension Railway in 1902. Although one example, No.1, was withdrawn as early as 1940 the remaining three lasted until 1953/4 when the L&LSR closed its railway operations.
Photo:
Mike Morant collection

Above
Pictured here on 29 June 1951 is Dingle, the south-western terminus of the Tralee & Dingle Light Railway. The pair of 2-6-0Ts (Nos. 1T and 2T) are seen after arrival at the end of their 31¼ mile journey from Tralee with the monthly cattle train. Both locomotives were built by the Hunslet Engine Co. in 1889.
Photo: Ivo Peters

Left
County Donegal Railways Joint Committee railcars Nos.19 & 20 are pictured during a busy period of activity at Donegal station on 8 June 1957. The railcars utilised Walker Bros chassis equipped with Gardner 6LW diesel engines and bodywork constructed by the GNR(I) Dundalk Works. They often ran with trailing vans, as evidenced here. After closure of the CDRJC system in 1959 the railcars were sold to the Isle of Man Railway – see page 67.
*Photo:
Transport Treasury*

Strabane & Letterkenny Railway.) All railways that were situated completely in the Irish Free State were amalgamated, in 1925, into the Great Southern Railway. A further consolidation of the Irish transport system took place in 1945 to form Coras Iompair Eireann (CIE).

Of the railway companies in the Republic of Ireland the **County Donegal Railways Joint Committee** eventually accounted for over 120 miles of running lines. It was the most extensive narrow gauge passenger system in the British Isles and in 1930 became the first to employ diesel motive power in regular use.

The CDRJC was formed jointly in 1906 by the Great Northern Railway of Ireland and the Midland Railway of England, inheriting 106 miles of lines including the Finn Valley Railway (Strabane to Stranorlar), West Donegal Railway (Stranorlar to Donegal) and those of the The Donegal Railway Company (Stranorlar to Glenties, Donegal Town to Killybegs, Strabane to Derry, and Donegal Town to Ballyshannon). The CDRJC went on to open the Strabane & Letterkenny Railway in 1909, bringing the total mileage for the CDRJC to 121. By 1912 the company possessed 21 locomotives, 56 passenger vehicles and 304 goods vehicles.

The Glenties branch closed in 1947, with the Strabane to Derry line following in 1954. The remaining passenger services ceased at the end of 1959, complete closure of most of the remaining lines coming in 1960.

The **Schull & Skibbereen Tramway & Light Railway** came into being following the granting of Parliamentary approval for the West Carbery Tramway & Light Railway Company to build a roadside tramway from the coastal terminus at Schull (on the waters of Roaringwater Bay) to the market town of Skibbereen (where it connected with the standard gauge), passing through the village of Ballydehob. The County Cork tramway, which ran for 15½ miles, was completed in 1886, but due to imperfections in its construction, it did not fully open until January 1888.

Having failed to make a profit in its first five years of operation, a Committee of Management was appointed by the local councils to oversee the running of the railway. As a result, the railway's name changed to the more familiar title of the S&ST&LR.

Following coal shortages after WW2, together with competition from road transport, the decision was taken to 'temporarily close' the railway in December 1946, but it was never to re-open. However, a visit to Skibbereen by the well known photographer, Ivo Peters, on 3 July 1950 was rewarded with the sight of one of the railway's locomotives (0-4-4T No.6s built by Thomas Green & Son), in steam specially for the late Irish railway enthusiast, C L Fry.

The **Tralee & Dingle Light Railway** opened in 1891 and ran for a distance of 31¼ miles, tracing a route south west from Tralee in County Kerry through the remote and rugged Dingle Peninsula to the town of Dingle, purported to be the most westerly railway station in Europe. There were severe gradients – with sections as steep as 1:29 – either side of the route's summit at Glenagalt, which stood 684' above sea level. Much of the route ran alongside a road, whilst at Tralee the line ran through the streets to reach the standard gauge goods yard where there were exchange sidings.

There used to be a six-mile branch from the main running line at Castlegregory Junction, running north west to Castlegregory, but this closed in 1939 around the same time as the cessation of passenger services. Daily freight workings operated thereafter, but from 1947 this was reduced to just a monthly cattle train, operated to coincide with the Dingle Fair and was usually double-headed. However, this infrequent use of the railway proved grossly uneconomic and the line closed completely in June 1953. One of the railway's iconic fleet of 2-6-0Ts, built by the Hunslet Engine Co., is preserved.

There are several organisations in Ireland that have been established to preserve parts of former narrow gauge lines, including the West Clare Railway and the Tralee & Blennerville Steam Railway, the latter operating along a short stretch of the former T&DLR route (although at the time of writing, services have been suspended).

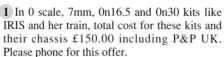
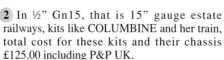
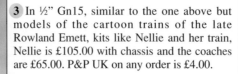
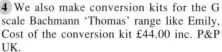

www.narrowplanet.co.uk

Custom etched nameplates, number plates and works plates for 4mm
to 16mm (and now 7/8":ft) scales, configured to your needs. Full range listed online.

From our own 009 range. We combine 3D printed body shells with etched
nickel silver details to create well detailed, easy to build kits.

NPL-001
99hp Baguley-Drewry

NPR-002
RNAD crew van

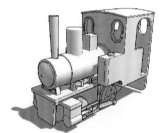

NPL-003
40hp O&K

Meridian Models plastic rolling stock kits. We also stock 009 kits by EuroNG,
Small Run Batch, Mosskito NG, Neil Sayer and Boston Largs Works.

MPM1 Ashover Light Railway coach

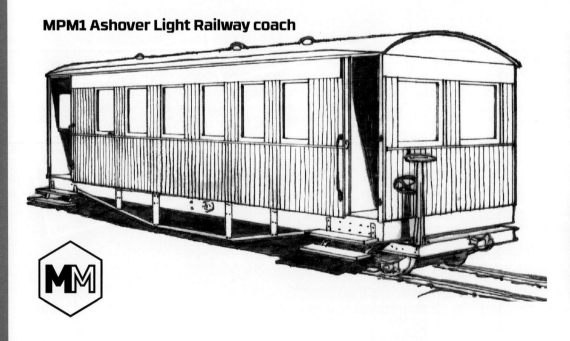

MPM8 Penrhyn fullersite wagon

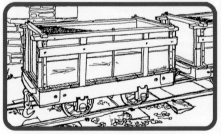

MPM10 Penrhyn coal wagon

PO Box 297, Bexhill-on-Sea, East Sussex, TN40 9HF • info@narrowplanet.co.uk

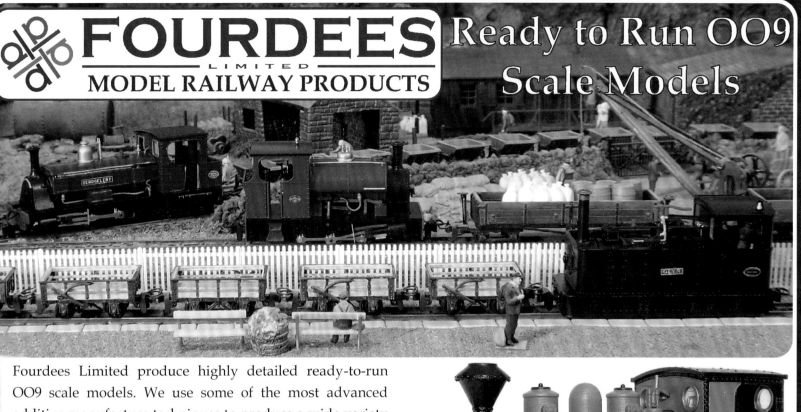

Chapter 4

Narrow gauge railways overseas

The use of narrow gauge tracks for railway routes spread across the world for the same reasons as made them useful in Britain – lower cost of construction and equipment, and the ability to cope with difficult terrain where sharper curves and steeper gradients were necessary.

Further, narrow gauge railways were eminently suitable for light traffic in thinly-populated areas where they provided a stimulus to industrial and commercial development, especially in the exploitation of natural resources in previously inaccessible locations, providing access to ports and standard gauge lines for onward transhipment.

Above
China: a C2 0-8-0 with a mixed train on the 760mm gauge Shibanxi colliery line, 3/11/03.
Photo: Rob Dickinson

Right
Czech Republic: 760mm gauge 0-6-2T U37 002 and Px48 0-8-0 at Jindrichuv Hradec, 23/8/10.
Photo: Blair Hobson

Above
Switzerland: SEFT metre gauge railcar No.3 at Cama on the Misoxerbahn / Ferrovie Mesolcine, 22/9/02.
Photo: Michael Farr

Above right
India: 2'6" gauge 1930-built Drewry railbus at Shimla on the Kalka – Shimla hill railway, 15/2/13.
Photo: Murray Reid

They could also be of strategic significance, and hence were often associated with a colonial power. The equipment was usually – at least initially – sourced from the 'home' country. In the early days there was some use of standard designs, so similar equipment could be seen in different places and countries, but specifications were soon adapted or converted to suit local conditions in the light of experience. Later there could be an interesting mix of influences, especially when local manufacturing capabilities were developed.

The world over

Overseas narrow gauge railways ranged from localised self–contained agricultural and industrial applications to main line common carriers, with extensive networks traversing long distances. There is a wide variety of gauges, and loading gauges, up to metre and 3'6", with motive power and rolling stock in some cases built to a loading gauge larger than that of standard gauge stock in the UK.

The problems of interchange with the standard gauge were avoided in some places as the whole network was built to narrow gauge specifications. In many places, especially the densely–populated and prosperous parts of Europe, the rise of road transport replaced the function of local light lines, but elsewhere main railway connections are still narrow gauge.

To cover overseas narrow gauge railways fully within the confines of this book is an impossible task, so, starting overleaf, we have prepared a snapshot of what could and can still be found operating on a continent by continent basis.

Above
Hungary: 760mm gauge C50 four-wheel forestry diesel hauling a bogie coach on the Balatonfenyves line in May 2005. *Photo: Myles Munsey*

Below
Austria: 760mm gauge – StLB Kh101 0-10-0T crossing the Ziller bridge near Zell am Ziller with a special train following overhaul in the Zillertalbahn workshops, 8/11/09.
Photo: Dr Markus Sträßle

Switzerland

Europe

France – *60cm and metre gauge secondary lines once served large parts of the country.*

Belgium – *metre gauge Vicinal.*

The Netherlands – *1,067mm tramways, plus some 60cm and 70cm.*

Germany – *750mm and metre widely used for light railways (Kleinbahnen); some quite extensive networks, perhaps most notably the Harz (metre) and Saxony (750mm) of which sections are still in use today as heritage lines.*

Austria – *760mm spread through the Austro–Hungarian empire, hence also in Hungary, Czechoslovakia, and Jugoslavia.*

Switzerland – *secondary railways almost all metre gauge; early users of electric power; much in evidence today. Rhätische Bahn is largest and best known.*

Italy – *950mm gauge in mountain regions, Sicily, and Sardinia.*

Greece – *metre gauge in the Peloponnese and Thessaly, 60cm east of Volos.*

Cyprus – *2'6" classic British colonial railway.*

Spain – *metre gauge along northern coast; metre and 750mm in Catalonia and Mediterranean coast.*

Sweden – *891mm (three Swedish feet).*

Norway – *started with 3'6".*

Poland – *60cm, 750mm, and metre all employed.*

Russia and Baltic states – *less known, but considerable use of 750mm for minor railways.*

Mountain rack railways were mostly narrow gauge although outside the scope of this short survey.

Above

Switzerland: on the metre gauge Rhätische Bahn, a new ABe8/12 'Allegra' three-unit railcar shows its capabilities hauling five coaches and a bogie wagon loaded with timber heading south approaching Bernina Suot, 21/6/11.
Photo: Jonathan Collinge

Below

The Netherlands: outside the new shed at the Stoomtrein Valkenburgse Meer site near Leiden (70cm gauge) are two former industrial 0-4-0Ts – Henschel No.8 and Orenstein & Koppel No.4. 29/9/12.
Photo: Dirk Schambach

Netherlands

Germany

Right
Germany: 750mm gauge – double departure from Bertsdorf on the Zittauer Schmalspurbahnen. On the left, IVK 145 makes for Kurort Jonsdorf, while 2-10-2T 99 749 on the right is bound for Kurort Oybin. 2/12/12. The line is one of several in Saxony still with steam services year round as part of the local public transport offering.
Photo: Matthias Altmann

Below
Austria: metre gauge Stern + Hafferl bogie electric railcar 26 111 with coach 228 at Attersee on the line from Vöcklamarkt. 9/7/09.
Photo: Ernst Leutwiler

Austria

Below
France: classic metre gauge – Vivarais 0-6-6-0T Mallet No.413 (Société Alsacienne 1932) heads a train over the tall viaduct at le Banchet, 19/5/00. French secondary lines often involved major civil engineering works and impressive structures.
Photo: M E Heath

France

Americas

Peru

Americas

USA and Mexico – *3' gauge was used to open up the country, and though much was subsequently converted to standard gauge when traffic developed a lot remained and some is now preserved, notably Durango & Silverton and Cumbres & Toltec. There were also 2' gauge lines in Maine.*

Canada – *3'6" in Newfoundland.*
Ecuador and Peru – *3' gauge.*
Brazil – *metre, 760mm, and 60cm.*
Argentina – *metre, and 750mm in Patagonia (Esquel, Rio Turbio).*

Left
Peru: 3' gauge Alco Co-Co diesel No.400 and railcar No.216 on the remote line from Cuzco which serves Machu Picchu, 2/11/13.
Photo: Bill Longley-Cook

Below
USA: an American 3' gauge classic – the narrow gauge train in the main street at Silverton, Colorado, upper terminus of the Durango & Silverton branch of the former Denver & Rio Grande Western. K36 2-8-2 No.482 has reversed the whole train on the wye in the nearby depot in readiness for the return trip. 13/9/2011.
Photo: Steve Flint

USA

USA

Right
USA: another classic American 3' gauge image – a geared loco and a trestle bridge. three-cylinder three-truck Shay No.9 ex-West Side Lumber Company on the high Devil's Gate Bridge on the Georgetown Loop tourist line in Colorado, 19/9/13.
Photo: Graham Lightfoot

Below right
Patagonia, Argentina: on 'La Trochita', the 750mm gauge line south from Inginiero Jacobacci to Esquel, Baldwin 2-8-2 No.3 bursts out of a tunnel. November 2007.
Photo: Bill Longley-Cook

Patagonia

Thailand

China

Above
Thailand: metre gauge – two 1995/6-built General Electric diesels in a tropical setting, Bang Sue shed, 10/2/13.
Photo: Terry Page

Below
China: local passenger hauled by a C2 0-8-0 o 760mm gauge Shibanx colliery railway, 11/6/0
Photo: Rob Dickinson

Right
India: a diesel-hauled regular train on the 2'6" gauge Kangara Valley line, 12/3/08.
Photo: Nick Dodson

India

Africa, Asia, and Australia

Africa – *metre gauge in east Africa, 3'6" in southern Africa, 2' in Namibia and South Africa, Sierra Leone 2'6", and Nigeria 3'6".*

India – *metre gauge (which might be considered odd for a former British colony), 2'6" for minor railways, 2' for hill railways, famously the Darjeeling Himalaya.*

China – *750mm gauge local lines, most developed in connection with industry, not widely known until recently*

Japan – *Main lines 3'6", some minor lines 750mm, also industrial systems.*

Indonesia – *Sugar cane and palm oil plantations, many different gauges.*

Australia – *3'6" essentially main line networks in Queensland, South Australia, Northern Territory, Western Australia, Tasmania (though 2' gauge on west coast serving mining and logging). 2'6" in Victoria (four lines, famously the Puffing Billy is preserved). 2' in Queensland for the sugar industry; also Fiji.*

New Zealand – *3'6" was used for the country's main line network.*

Right
India: for much of its length as it climbs into the hills, the 2' gauge Darjeeling Himalaya Railway is close to the Hill Cart Road. 4/4/13.
Photo: Nick Dodson

Below
Australia: Queensland 2' gauge – Colonial Sugar Refining Macknade Mill 0-6-0 No.6 (Hudswell Clarke 1862 of 1953) draws loaded bins between fields of young and mature cane in the last year of steam. 24/8/76.
Photo: Ken Walker

India

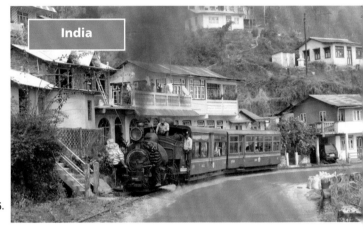

Australia

Modelling overseas narrow gauge

The enthusiast who takes an interest in foreign narrow gauge lines has a far greater choice of ready–to–run equipment than his British modelling counterpart. This is one reason why many settle for an overseas project, and the choice of scale and gauge is far greater, as the accompanying table shows.

Apart from the well–known European suppliers noted in the table, narrow gauge models have also been the preserve of low volume short run specialists, often as kits, or brass models built in batches, and for local markets. There have been far too many to list, and not all are still active.

With such a worldwide presence and choice, it is no surprise that narrow gauge features regularly in CONTINENTAL MODELLER and to give you a flavour of the types of layouts that can be constructed we have included a selection in the pages which follow.

Overseas loco and stock

As an aside, the use in the UK of overseas narrow gauge locomotive and rolling stock designs was not common in the heyday of British narrow gauge, but neither was it unknown: for example, the Baldwin 2-4-2T *Lyn* on the Lynton & Barnstaple, and former War Department Baldwins and Alcos on the Ashover, Snailbeach, Welsh

Above left
Rio Grande Southern,
On30 by Tony Morris.
CM September 2011.
Photos: Steve Flint

Right
Tuscarora Mine,
On30 by John Green.
CM November 2007.

Manufacturer	Railways of	Scale/gauge
Egger/Playcraft/Jouef	France and Germany	HOe
Liliput	Austria	HOe
Roco	Austria, Germany	HOe
Bemo	Germany	HOe & HOm
Bemo	Switzerland	HOm
Technomodell (now pmt)	Germany, specifically Saxony	HOe
Tillig	Germany, developing Harz range	HOm & HOe
Busch	Germany, Feldbahn (industrial/agricultural)	HOf
Minitrains	America, more recently also Europe	HOn30, HOe
Bemo	Switzerland (new range being developed)	Om
Bachmann Spectrum	America (a considerable range)	On30
Broadway Limited Imports	America	On30
Mountain Model Imports	America	On30
Haskell	Victorian 'Puffing Billy' 2-6-2T	On30
Ixion	South Australian 'Coffee Pot' steam railcar	On30
LGB	German, Switzerland, and America	G
Bachmann	America and others	G
Piko	America and Germany	G
Accucraft	America and others	G

Above
Zauberwaldbahn, Oe
by Norton Cross MRG.
CM January 2011.

Right and below
Bierdorf, HOe
by Roger Nicholls.

Highland, Glyn Valley,
and Penrhyn quarry sys-
tem.

With the rush to preservation in
the latter half of the 20th century, and
equipment being returned from overseas, much
was acquired for use on British preserved lines while
still available cheaply. UK railways which run overseas outline
stock include the Welshpool and Llanfair, Welsh Highland Railway,
West Lancashire Light Railway, Bredgar & Wormshill and the private system
at Statfold Barn, amongst others.

The result is that British narrow gauge layouts can easily justify the use of foreign
stock; in fact, British modellers have long been using 'anglicised' versions of commercially available models of overseas prototypes.

Pfaffenbrücke

Austrian HOe

Layout information in brief

Austrian HOe by Howard and Eileen Lawrence
Location: based on the Ybbstalbahn Bergstrecke
Period: variable
Size: 4' x 2' scenic section plus fiddle yards
Control: DC
Stock: Liliput, Roco, Narobahn, Stängl
See CM September 2009.

CF de Ventoux

French HOm

Layout information in brief

French HOm by Richard Lane
Location: south of France
Period: 1990s and later
Size: 16'6" x 8'
Control: DC
Stock: mostly scratchbuilt or adapted from commercial items
See CM December 2008, January 2009, May 2009, July 2011

Zauberwaldbahn

German Oe

Layout information in brief

German Oe by Norton Cross MRG
Location: Brandenburg, East Germany
Period: 1960s
Size: 12' x 3'4"
Control: DC
Stock: mostly adapted from Fleischmann
'Magic Train' commercial items
See CM January 2011

Rio Grande Southern

American On30

Layout information in brief

American On30 by Tony Morris
Location: Colorado Rockies
Period: 1940s-1950s
Size: 24' x 12'
Control: DCC
Stock: mostly Bachmann Spectrum,
plus Broadway Limited Imports and MMI
See CM September 2011

FC Eldorado

Mexican On30

Layout information in brief

Mexican On30 by Roger Nicholls
Location: gold mine in northern Mexico
Period: 1930s
Size: 6' x 2'
Control: DC
Stock: mostly adapted from commercial Bachmann items
See CM March 2006

Rest of the world

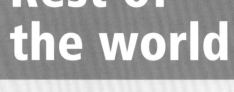

Argentina
1:87 stock by Davide Raseni

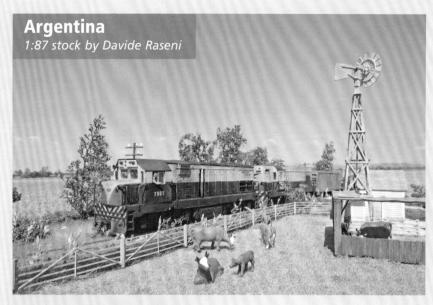

Nilgiri, India
1:87 stock by Warren Miller

Janakpur, Nepal
HOe by Roderik Vanderkelen

< South Africa
1:87 by Ulrich Slovig

Pabrik Gula Jairuba
Java, HOe by Diger Rossel

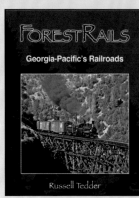

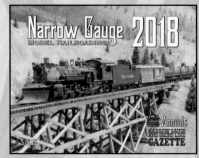

NGTrains.com
EDM Models on the Web

CATEGORIES

Steam Locomotives
Diesel Locomotives
Railcars & Speeders
Passenger Cars
Freight Cars
Trucks & Couplers
Track & Rail
Decals
Detail Parts

MANUFACTURERS

Accucraft
Banta Models
Blackstone Models
Blue Point
EDM Models
Evergreen Hill
Foothill Models
Haskell
Ixion Models
Kadee
Magic Water
Maiten Shops
Minerva Models
Mount Blue Models
Mountain Blue Figures
Mt Albert
NCE
Port Wynnstay
Precision Scale Co
San Juan Car
San Juan Decals
Sculptamold
Soundtraxx
Wuiske QR Models
ZIMO

OUR OWN RANGE OF KITS

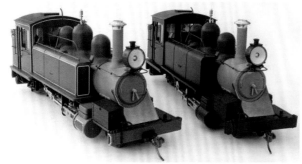

READY TO RUN MODELS   INTERNATIONAL NG MODELS

NARROW GAUGE PUBLICATIONS

EDM Models

19 Briar Avenue, Acomb, York YO26 5BX
01904 331973   info@ngtrains.com
www.ngtrains.com

Chapter 5

Narrow gauge in the garden

OUTDOOR NARROW GAUGE RAILWAYS ARE GREAT FUN TO CREATE AND RELAXING TO OPERATE ON FINE SUMMER DAYS, BUT HOW DO YOU SET ABOUT CONSTRUCTING YOUR OWN? **ANDREW AND JOSEPH BEARD**, WHO BUILT ONE AROUND THEIR FAMILY GARDEN, OFFER SOME HELPFUL ADVICE ON THE TOPIC.

PHOTOS BY CRAIG TILEY OR AS CREDITED

Model narrow gauge garden railways broadly fall into two groups, these being G scale and SM32 scale. There are of course variations on these which will be mentioned later. G scale is modelled at 1:22.5 which works out at 13.5mm:1' and uses a track gauge of 45mm. SM32 is modelled at 1:19 which works out at 16mm:1' and uses a track gauge of 32mm.

Design considerations

By way of an introduction it is probably best to start with the track base or baseboard as these are common to either scale. When designing a garden railway it is important to take into account the area in which the railway is to be built, taking note of any slopes in the terrain, immovable objects such as sheds, large trees, footpaths etc and to plan accordingly. Firstly it is a good idea to draw a scale plan of the garden area marking in all the above, ideally dividing the plan into 12" squares (or 300mm if you work in metric) to assist with the layout design process. At this stage it is useful to make a number of photocopies on which to sketch some layout designs and ideas.

Minimum track radii must be taken into account at the design stage to ensure the curves will be suitable for the locomotives and stock that you plan to run. Most G scale stock can run on curves as tight as 24" (600mm), but it is always best to check if you have a particularly large loco-motive in mind to ensure it will cope with the curves, and also to have adequate clearance around fixed items like trees. With SM32 the minimum suggested radius, especially where you wish to run steam powered locomotives, would be 2'6" (750mm), but again if you are planning on buying larger locomotives then a larger radius is best. Either way the larger the radius the better, as this will allow for smoother running, and avoids stock overhanging on tight curves which can look rather odd. Unless you have a partic-

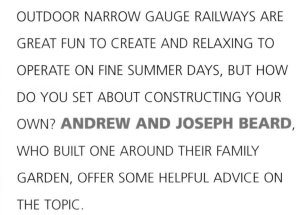

Left
An Accucraft Ragleth class locomotive (radio-controlled live steam) on Andrew and Joseph's SM32 garden railway system.

ularly small area to use, a larger layout is better and will give the trains somewhere to go to and return from. Most importantly you will need to decide if the layout is solely for your own use, or will you be hosting meetings for friends to run their trains as well? If you intend hosting meetings, then it is worth considering where all the extra locomotives and stock will be placed and how the layout can be operated with multiple trains in action, so adding some double track or passing loops is almost essential plus of course plenty of siding space for storing rolling stock. The plus side of course is that when everyone else has gone home, you have a more interesting layout to operate. For live steam operation, a steaming-up/servicing area is essential to avoid conflict with trains running on the main layout.

Raised and ground level trackbeds

With a basic plan arrived at it is a good idea to plot out the route in the garden using simple wooden pegs tapped into the ground to give an overall idea of how the design would appear. Of course it is also important to consider at what height you would like your layout to be. Many garden railway enthusiasts have their own preference, whether it be a ground level line or a raised one, and these both have their pros and cons.

A ground level line can blend seamlessly into the garden environment, but can be prone to flooding in low lying areas of garden unless adequately drained. Also the local wildlife will soon take a keen interest in your creation, and will be rooting around in the borders and depositing debris on the line. Of course leaves on the line in the autumn are an issue, but for the determined enthusiast, a quick whip-round with a soft handbrush will soon clear the line for a running session. Another thing to bear in mind with a ground level line is that you will need to bend down quite a bit to tend to your layout and trains, which as most of us will testify can be an issue. For a raised line, bending down is

not an issue so much, as a different form of construction is required to give a stable trackbed, but at least the garden borders won't end up on the trackbed, although leaves will still cause an autumnal problem of course.

Many gardens are rarely completely level so a combination of ground level and raised trackbed is quite common and can look more natural. Whichever type you choose, it is best to have the steaming up/servicing area at waist height as it is much easier to work on your locomotive. On our line at home, much of the trackbed is raised, with a lowered walking/standing area in the servicing area, but due to the changes in height in the garden, part of the trackbed is almost at ground level, so with careful choice of plants/bushes the whole blends together after a short while. The sunken floor of the servicing area has generous amounts of gravel drainage, but can still flood to a depth of several inches during heavy rain, but then again if that happens we will be indoors having a cup of tea, so once the rain stops this area soon drains away ready for use again.

Trackbed construction

There are many types of base that can be used for the track to be laid on, and it seems that new ideas pop up from time to time as well. For a ground level line some may consider using a concreted base, or breeze blocks laid flat, and

Above
An example of a raised trackbed on supports made from fence posts.

Top left
A view of the *Vale of Evermore Railway*, Keith Skillicorn's ground level system in SM32, which was featured in the September 2014 RM. *Photo: Derek Shore*

Bottom left
Nick Colthorpe tends to a locomotive in the servicing area on the outdoor system at Pecorama. *Photo: Dave Clements*

Below
Joseph Beard fills a locomotive with butane in the servicing area of their layout. Note how the ground level has been lowered.

these are both ideal where the layout is to be permanent. Fixing the track in place can be somewhat more labour intensive though, as track will need to be screwed down into previously Rawplugged holes which will need to be drilled at regular intervals into the base. Leaving the track free-floating in these scales is not really an option as there is not sufficient weight in the track to make sure it stays put. A raised structure is usually, but not exclusively, built of timber. For the uprights on our railway we used 4" wooden fence posts concreted in place with 2" x 1" tannalised timbers screwed to the side of the posts at the required height to give a skeleton structure for the baseboard. For the baseboard surface we used decking timber, smooth side up, screwed to the outer timbers.

Other methods of construction that have been used involve stone or brick piers or walls such as on the layout at Pecorama, while other lines have used steel posts and framework, or even plastic drainpipe for the uprights. Whichever method you use, take your time over construction to get a smooth layout base with no humps and bumps or odd cambers, as this will pay dividends when your track is laid and you start running trains. Returning to the raised construction, the baseboard can be left as it is if you wish or, as many modellers do, you can cover the boards with smooth roofing felt secured at the outer edges with roofing felt nails to give an imitation ballasted look. To neaten up the edges it is best to add tannalised timber strips over the felt edges which helps hold it in place, but also looks much tidier.

Other types of baseboard material that can be used are marine plywood (hard to find and also expensive), and recycled plastic boards made to look like timber boards which of course will not rot. Of all the types of baseboard top, decking timber is the easiest to source and probably the most cost effective. With all of these types of surface, track can simply be pinned in place using brass nails. It is of course possible to add real stone ballast, and we have found that the most long lasting method of securing it is to use exterior grade PVA. The glue is applied neat and the stone ballast is carefully sprinkled in place before being pressed into the glue using a small wooden stick. On a ground level line ballasting can be done using a cement/sand/ballast mix which is applied dry before being

wetted using a watering can fitted with a fine rose. So whatever track/ballast combination you decide on it is very much each to their own, and after all we are after the essence of trains running through a garden landscape rather than finescale modelling.

For a raised layout the extra building work can seem daunting, and to some will look like trains running on stilts, but by careful planning even this can be incorporated into the overall scene. Adding bridges in strategic places adds a feeling of the layout being part of the landscape, and the use of slow growing hedging will hide the structure. We used Euonymus and Box hedging, which are both slow growing, and only require trimming a couple of times a year. For all the ideas on building the layout base that we have mentioned, there are no doubt many more and indeed garden railway enthusiasts are a resourceful crowd who often find uses for products not previously considered suitable for garden railways.

Laying the track

Track in both G gauge and SM32 is available from Peco, both as sectional Setrack and also flexible track. It is important to ensure that the track is well laid, to avoid expensive locomotives and stock from derailing and being damaged. A usual starting place for tracklaying would be at a point or group of points with the plain track being laid away from this area, fixing the track as you go. It is helpful to make some preset radii wooden curves to assist with laying curves, and these can be made from offcuts of plywood or hardboard, using a simple pencil and string approach to draw out the required radii. Cutting the curve is best done using a jigsaw. Before you start laying curved sections of track it is helpful to pre-curve some pieces of flexible track so that you can avoid dogleg joints where one piece of curved track joins to another.

To do this in either G gauge or SM32 you should slide the rail out of the railchairs by about 6" and then carefully pre-curve the rail in the direction required using your fingers if it is a gentle curve, or with pliers for a sharper radius. The rail can then be fed back through the railchairs, before the next rail is similarly curved. The finished section of flexible track will then have curves at both ends with a straight section in the middle, but is otherwise ready to lay. Small

Above
Sections of Ian Gurr's outdoor railway are supported by a stone trackbed, as illustrated here. The locomotive is a radio-controlled live steam Welshpool & Llanfair 2-4-0T, manufactured by Accucraft.

Top left
Bridges provide a means of visually breaking up continuous expanses of raised trackbed. This structure is on Andrew and Joseph's garden railway. The locomotive is based on a Ffestiniog Railway George England & Co. 0-4-0STT, built from scratch using IP Engineering chassis and cylinder components.

Right
Gareth Jones' *Hope Mountain Railway* (featured in the September 2013 RM) is a magnificent example of what can be achieved with an outdoor system in SM32. The majority of the railway is supported on cast concrete beams, but there are sections constructed from wooden decking with brick pier legs.
Photo: Gareth Jones

Above
The outdoor SM32 system at Pecorama features ballasted trackwork, undertaken using garden grit, fixed in place with PVA.
Photo: Dave Clements

lot of extra work to put things right. Tracklaying should continue around the circuit, and you will find it is easiest to make the final connection on a straight rather than on a curve. As you lay the curved track you will notice the inner rail overlapping the outer one, and this can be cut off square before connecting on the next piece of track, or when you get more experienced at tracklaying it is possible to make a staggered joint which will give a smoother join. Either way use the pre-set wooden curves held against the inner or outer rail to help maintain a smooth, constant radius.

One other thing to check as you are laying the track is the level across the rails. I use a short pocket size spirit level for this, the aim being to have the straight track perfectly level with the bubble of the level bang in the middle. For curves it is useful to introduce a small amount of cant or superelevation so that the train leans into the curve for a smoother run. Using the spirit level we want the bubble slightly off centre on a curve with the outer rail raised above the inner rail by approx. 1mm. To keep the track in this position, small squares of styrene sheet can be used as packing under the outer sleeper ends. We found it useful to have a selection of thicknesses ranging from 20thou to 60thou to hand to give the required amount of cant. Ideally the packing should be fixed in place so that it cannot fall out or become dislodged.

As tracklaying proceeds, it is handy to have a couple of items of rolling stock to test the newly laid track so that any adjustments can be made before proceeding further. When you are laying track from a straight to a curve, don't

blind holes are moulded on the underside ends of the sleepers which will need drilling through with a small drill bit to accommodate the screws/nails, before tracklaying can commence.

Being outdoors, the rails will expand and contract with varying temperatures so it is important to leave a gap between the rail ends at every joint of approx. 1/8" (3mm) for expansion room. Yes, the rails really can expand this much on a hot summer day. Tightly butting the rail ends together is to be avoided, because when the rails expand on a sunny day the track has nowhere to go except up or sideways which will inevitably lead to derailments and a

forget to add a short transition curve, which will give a smooth transition for trains from straight to curved track. Basically this is the straight gradually becoming a curve before it becomes the actual radius of the main curve. A transition curve will also look much better. The final sections of track to be laid are the passing loops and sidings. You will probably have a few short sections of track offcuts to hand by now, and these can be joined together in a couple of sidings to use up the odds and ends, and is exactly what would have happened on real railways. Points are usually operated by hand, but some modellers do operate them with electrically powered point motors, and there has also been a pneumatic system used, although this is possibly not currently available.

Essential wiring outdoors

So with all your track laid it is best to test the whole layout. In SM32 scale you could use a simple battery powered test locomotive or your steam locomotive and if all is satisfactory you are ready to start running trains, but if you are using G gauge track powered locos you will need to connect up a controller to the track to do this. With a track pick-up powered layout (mostly confined to G gauge) it is important to consider the electrical aspect, as clearly a mains powered controller is not suitable for outdoor use. Many modellers will have a garden shed next to the layout to which mains power has been connected, and so the controller can be housed in there to keep it dry and safe.

Low voltage power from the controller to the track can be connected using multistrand wire of at least 16/0.2mm size, but ideally larger, with the track connection being a soldered one. The rail joiners outdoors are really only the physical connection and should not be relied upon for electrical continuity so a loop of wire needs to be soldered

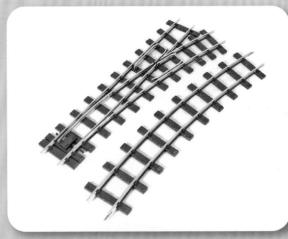

Left
Peco manufactures track components for both SM32 and G scales. The SM32 products (illustrated) utilise Code 200 rail and comprise flexible plain track, first and second radius curves, together with small and medium radius points (Electrofrog only). For G scale (Code 250 rail), there is flexible track, Setrack curves and straights, and medium radius points (Insulfrog only).
Photo: Jolyon Sargent

across at every rail joiner to give reliable connection of track power to all parts of the layout. Even points should be wired in this way to increase electrical reliability. The rail head will tarnish just as the rest of the rail will do, and whilst this will give a pleasing, weathered effect to the rail as a whole, it will not allow good electrical pick up by the locomotive through the wheels, so it will be necessary to clean the rail head surface with a track cleaning rubber to impart a shine so that trains can run. Many G gauge locomotives are fitted with extra skate pick-ups which run on the rail head which help with smooth running, and will also keep the surface of the rail cleaner, but if the layout is not used for longer periods then a spot of elbow grease will be required to get the track ready for a running session. The G gauge layout at Pecorama is in use every day from April to October so the track is kept usable by the trains being run regularly, however we have found that with locomotives that are not fitted with pick-up skates, then track cleaning is required on an occasional basis, but especially after we have had a period of rain.

To clean the rails we use Peco PL-41 rail

Below
Ian Gurr brings a Lynton & Barnstaple passenger train to a stop on his SM32 *Axe Valley Railway*. The use of L&B locomotives and stock – which are based on comparatively large prototypes – dictated a minimum radius of 4'6".

Right

This G Scale Lenz type i 0-4-0T is manufactured by LGB and represents a German metre gauge prototype. Of largely plastic construction, it features a sealed mechanism to suit outdoor use. It also features sprung shoes to provide additional electrical pick-up.

cleaners, but due to the gauge of the track being wider than the rail cleaner, we have pinned four of these to a block of wood in a two-by-two formation which makes rail cleaning much easier and quicker. When the cleaners wear out we just unpin them, turn them over and pin them back in place. A set of cleaners usually lasts us a whole season.

LOCOMOTIVES AND STOCK

G scale

The range of locomotives and stock has varied hugely over the years, and for those contemplating this scale will largely be confined to scale models of European and North American prototypes. There are a good number of manufacturers in this scale with the most well-known ones being LGB, Piko and Bachmann. All of these makes are ready-to-run, track powered, and can be used straight from the box. Some modellers prefer to run trains in this scale using radio control, and so in many cases they will convert their locomotives to on board battery power with r/c for direction and speed control, and in some cases digital sound units can be added for extra effects.

More details on the range of items available can be found on garden railway websites, but you could also consider joining the G Scale Society which has a very useful website – www.gscalesociety.com – on which will be found much useful information, plus it publishes a magazine four times a year with interesting articles and adverts. Members also benefit from public liability insurance for when they are operating their trains at a public-attended event.

SM32

If you prefer your trains to be British outline, then SM32 scale is for you. SM stands for 16mm:1' scale and 32 being the track gauge of 32mm, so this will mean locomotives and stock represented will be running on a scale 2' gauge track, although a degree of modellers' licence is generally allowed to cater for those lines that are/were slightly wider or narrower in gauge such as the Talyllyn Railway which is 2'3" gauge. Locomotives mainly fall into two groups, being battery powered or live steam.

Battery powered locomotives can be bought in kit form for an inexpensive and easy to build project, which gives the satisfaction of having something you have built yourself, running on the railway line that you have constructed. This is an excellent place to start and often your first battery powered loco will be used as a test loco for hauling newly built stock or indeed to check the line before the first run of the day with your steam powered locomotive. Of course it is also possible to buy bigger and more powerful battery powered engines in ready-to-run form, and if you wish they can be fitted with r/c and sound units, but naturally the cost will increase. These type of locomotives are in some cases quite capable of hauling a stranded out-of-steam locomotive back to the servicing area from the furthest reaches of your line, so can be considered a very useful back-up. They are also ideal for when you just want to pop into the garden for half-an-hour to run a train without wanting to get everything out to raise steam in your new steam locomotive.

Of course, nothing beats the sight and sound (and in the case of a coal fired engine, the smell) of a real steam powered locomotive, plus of course the thrill of driving your own locomotive. Steam powered locomotives generally come ready built and can be used straight from the box, once you have read and followed the operating instructions. They vary in price hugely, but a good starter locomotive, manually controlled, can be bought for less than £700, and adding r/c yourself, at a later date, is relatively cheap at under £100. A mid-priced locomotive with r/c already fitted will cost approx. £1500, whilst if you want a really large and powerful locomotive, such as the soon to be released gas fired Roundhouse model of the Darjeeling Garratt at £3550. Or even larger, a coal fired South African Railway's NG/G16 Garratt can be bought for £5450.

Above
A member of the locomotive fleet on Keith Skillicorn's *Vale of Evermore Railway*; a live-steam gas-fired model of Penrhyn Quarry Hunslet 0-4-0ST *Gwynedd*, manufactured by Finescale Engineering.
Photo: Derek Shore

Below
Proof that obtaining motive power for a garden railway doesn't need to be an expensive exercise; this diminutive vehicle was built by Andrew Beard from a modified IP Engineering kit. It is manually controlled and powered by two AAA batteries.

Many garden railway enthusiasts run their engines under manual control, i.e. raise steam, hook up a rake of stock and set the train going at a steady pace while they sit back with a brew to enjoy the sights and sounds as the train proceeds around their railway. However this only really works successfully on a line that is both level and has generous radius curves. My own railway has tighter radius curves, and while it is possible to run locos under manual control, they can sometimes stall on the curves if they do not have a sufficient head of steam, or are running just a bit too slowly, meaning that the 'hand from the sky' has to intervene. Better then to add radio control to some or all of your locomotives which gives a whole new driving experience, as you will actually be in constant control of your locomotive, plus it will allow you to stop at stations to collect passengers, or to indulge in a spot of shunting in the goods yard. The addition of r/c is relatively inexpensive and will convert a manual locomotive into a driveable machine, with the option of forward or reverse at the flick of a stick on the r/c controller. This will make the loco more suited to sharply curved parts of the track, but also where a line has gradients.

Most steam powered locomotives are butane gas fired, with an on board tank being filled from a standard cartridge (such as would be used for a blowtorch). Early SM32 locomotives were methylated spirits fired, usually with a simple pot boiler, and a chicken feed type meths tank supplying multiple burners.

The ultimate has to be a coal fired locomotive. Nothing can beat the smell of coal smoke lazily drifting across the garden as you raise steam on your pride of the line. These locomotives will of course cost more than a standard gas fired one, and are usually built to order in small batches by specialist manufacturers. On a coal fired locomotive, everything is in miniature from the firebox door to the shovel, and naturally the lumps of coal. Coal firing has, at times, been described as a bit of a dark art, but over the last few years this has changed with more manufacturers, and more garden railway enthusiasts willing to share their experiences and skills. Enhancements and detailing parts can be added to your locomotive, such as a steam powered whistle (from DJB Engineering), or a water top up system so that a loco can be kept in steam for longer periods.

Another innovation is a chuffer unit which fits onto the exhaust steam pipe in the chimney to enhance the chuff sound of your locomotive. It is a simple to fit unit and at £25 is an affordable addition. It is also very useful when your loco disappears behind bushes as you can tell where it is and how hard it is working. Some locomotives have re-gaugeable wheelsets that can be adjusted, so that you can run on another line which is to 45mm gauge.

So to sum up, steam locomotives can be bought from a large number of manufacturers such as Roundhouse Engineering, Accucraft, ELR Engineering, DJB Engineering, Riverdale, and Wrightscale to name just a few. Battery powered locos, kits and chassis are available from Roundhouse Engineering, Essel Engineering, IP Engineering, Yatton Engineering, Swift Sixteen and many more. A search through the links section on the 16mm Association of Railway Modellers website (see feature on pages 104 & 105) will provide much useful information.

Rolling stock

There are currently a few items of ready-to-run rolling stock in this scale, but most are built from readily available kits either in cast resin, laser cut wood, or precision cut wood. Assembly of these kits is straightforward and most will come with written instructions and illustrations/diagrams. Indeed some manufacturers now supply their instructions on CD. If you have built an Airfix kit then you can most certainly build a coach or wagon kit in this scale, it's just a bit bigger!

Some of you may wish to scratchbuild your stock which of course saves money, but not necessarily time as each part has to be cut to shape before being glued in place. Having said that it does allow the creation of scale models which are not available in kit form or if you just fancy building something a bit different or for a special purpose, such as a track cleaning wagon. A lot of my own stock is scratchbuilt, and quite apart from being cheaper, there is a tremendous sense of achievement at having built something to your own design.

Rolling stock kit providers are many and a look through the Association website or magazine will be found most useful. It should also be mentioned that many kits can be fitted with 45mm gauge wheelsets for those modellers who wish to run on G gauge track.

Narrow gauge in the garden

Above
The station on Andrew and Joseph's railway, showing the solar-powered platform lighting referred to in the text.

Top right
This bridge was constructed from aluminium angle, riveted together with a pop rivet tool.

Below
Sun, steam and shade – all combining to create an atmosphere that is only possible with an outdoor live steam system. A Roundhouse Leek & Manifold Kitson 2-6-4T arrives with a passenger train on Ian Gurr's *Axe Valley Railway*.

Lineside details and structures

A whole range of kits exist to whet the appetite, the handy thing being that as they are mostly generic designs and to narrow gauge size, they can just as easily be used for G scale or SM32. For buildings that live outdoors you will need those which are made in plastic or resin, although some kits are made using waterproof MDF which when painted can stay outdoors. Many detailing items are available from sacks and barrels to signs and figures with just about everything in between, but often it is about the modellers' ingenuity in using a totally unrelated item and converting it for garden railway use.

Take our station lamps for example. The lamps themselves are constructed out of brass tube and rod with a paint tin lid as the shade, but the best bit is that they actu-ally work! I adapted solar powered garden lights by care-fully removing the LED from the solar lamp and fitting these in the station lamps, with trailing wires running under the bushes to the original solar unit. They charge up by day, then automatically switch on at night to provide a pleasing light for any late night passengers at the station. A bit of a gimmick maybe, but great fun!

The bridge on our line is intended to be a feature and is made using aluminium angle and strip purchased from the local DIY shop, with it all being riveted together with a pop rivet tool. It cost probably £20 to make, but should last for years and will never rust.

AND FINALLY...

It is of course important to remember that your valuable locomotives and stock should be safely and securely stored. Although the passenger and goods stock can be locked away in a shed or garage, it is always advisable to store locomotives indoors, not only because of their value, but also to protect the steam powered ones from frost, as ice in a loco boiler could cause irreparable damage.

Above all though, garden railway modelling is intended to be both enjoyable and fun!

The Association of 16mm Narrow Gauge Modellers

As you read this in 2017 the Association of 16mm Narrow Gauge Modellers is 40 years old. From small beginnings in 1977, when three dozen modellers came together to form the Association, there is now a worldwide membership of some 4,500, with over 50 Area Groups, and the volunteers produce two quarterly full colour magazines and probably the largest annual garden railway show in the world.

What is 16mm?

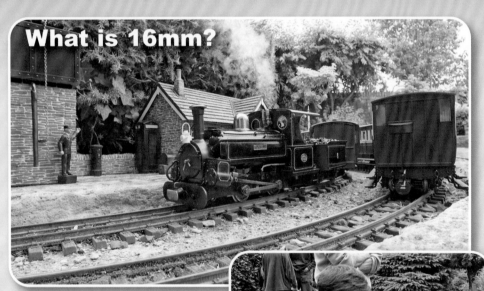

16mm scale models, especially those powered by live steam, have a special aura all their own.

Talking to people at events and exhibitions it can be surprising just how confusing matters such as scale and gauge can be, even to people who consider themselves to be railway modellers!

Modelling in the scale of 16mm to the foot, particularly for the operation of live steam in the garden, is probably as much about practicality as anything. Modelling in O gauge/7mm to the foot, using 32mm gauge track to represent standard gauge prototypes has been around for many decades, and track components were available both in kit form and products such as Peco Streamline, albeit with sleeper spacing and rail profile not entirely suited to narrow gauge modelling.

The advantages of taking this established gauge, but using a scale of 16mm to the foot and modelling narrow gauge prototypes, apart from the availability of existing components, and perhaps an existing line that could be adapted, were that cylinders could be bigger and offer a wider and more practical power band, yet remain close to scale, boilers could be larger, and as technology developed,

Checking a loco for fuel and water; members of the Association have regular 'get-togethers' at garden railways across the country.

the generally larger bodywork could better accommodate radio control and gas tanks for fuel.

Of course the fact that at 16mm to the foot 32mm gauge track represented 2' gauge track in the real world may well have been a factor in

popularising the scale too, since many of the early pioneers were also involved in projects with Welsh narrow gauge heritage railways as well!

However the Association is a broad church, and although the name has stuck, our members actually model in a range of scales between around 14mm to the foot and $7/8$" to the foot, with both 32mm and 45mm gauge track being commonly used. This in part reflects the rather flexible approach to scale of some commercial manufacturers over the years, but is also representative of the individuality of the narrow gauge prototype with a range of track gauges and approaches to loading gauge and the size of locomotives and rolling stock.

The essence of 16mm though is about running trains in the garden. Gas, coal or meths fired, sometimes battery electric, there are even people who have real diesel powered locos!

Being narrow gauge, tight radii and short trains can be the norm, so even the small gardens associated with modern British homes can accommodate a perfectly respectable layout, and with a range of kits and ready-to-run components from track to live steam locos available from a growing list of suppliers, at reasonable prices you don't have to be an engineer, country landowner nor win the lottery to get into 16mm railway modelling.

If you want to get an idea of how this all comes together then take a look at the Association's website www.16mm.org.uk where there are loads of pictures and videos showing 16mm members and their trains in action.

The website provides a host of other information too including links to suppliers, details of the Association's Local Area Groups across the UK and around the world, and a UK events diary.

Where to see 16mm in action ...

16mm isn't just a garden scale; many of our members have indoor layouts too, ranging from a bit of test track to fully scenic exhibition standard lines.

Believed to be the biggest event of its kind in the world, the National Garden Railway Show is the Association's annual event, attracting all the major manufacturers, and often used as a platform for new product launches, the show also showcases the vast range of 16mm Association modelling with layouts, demonstrations and examples of the modellers' art in the Model of the Year competition.

The show usually takes place at the end of March or beginning of April – see www.nationalgardenrailwayshow.org.uk for details

If you can't make the National Show then 16mm scale layouts are increasingly featured at other model railway shows and there are a number of dedicated garden scale shows, in particular the annual Elsecar Garden Railway Show, run by the Yorkshire Group of the 16mm Association and usually taking place at the end of September at the Elsecar Heritage Centre.

Details of this show and other events where 16mm models can be seen in action can be found in the diary section of www.16mm.org.uk. There are also a number of UK Heritage Railways with well established 16mm layouts such as the Midland Railway – Butterley, The Severn Valley and Talyllyn.

At a recent Derbyshire open gardens event, one of the most popular was the one with a 16mm scale railway in it!

"You don't need to be a country landowner to get into 16mm railway modelling" – a Roundhouse Lady Anne in action on the Inham Valley Railway.

Garden railways can be operated all year round – this John Prescott Wagtail class engine gets to grips with wintry conditions.

One of the many freelance designs or model of a real thing, such as this Vale of Rheidol 2-6-2T – take your pick!

Benefits of 16mm Association Membership in a nutshell

- Access to years of 16mm modelling experience – help and advice willingly given.
- Join a growing network of over 4,000 members worldwide.
- A copy of the latest New Members Guide to modelling in 16mm narrow gauge, with 64 pages of colour pictures, diagrams and text giving invaluable advice.
- 16mm Today – a high quality full colour magazine every quarter, packed with modelling information and advice.
- Bulletin – the Association's full colour quarterly members' newsletter with details of events, area group activities and local garden railway meetings, plus a members' sales and wanted section, where you can find some real bargains.
- A vibrant network of Local Area Groups.
- Full public liability insurance cover for members' garden railway meetings and live steam locomotives.
- National Garden Railway Show every spring.
- Junior modellers network for U18 with online and face-to-face activities
- Family/Associate membership
- A lot of satisfaction and enjoyment!

Join online today at www.16mm.org.uk

Chapter 6

Modelling projects

Although the range of ready-to-run items in the popular narrow gauge scale/gauge combinations is increasing – not least in OO9 – there is still a need for kitbuilding and scratchbuilding models. Indeed, this is how many of the scale/gauge combinations were derived; modellers took proven mechanisms and worked to the desired gauge that the chassis represented. Thus when TT came along, the possibilities for using 12mm gauge models to represent 3' gauge prototypes in 4mm scale were suddenly opened wide. In the same vein, when N gauge was developed, the whole scope for using its mechanisms to represent the approximately 2'6" gauge prototypes (OO9) was widened.

Notwithstanding the fact that there are some highly-crafted and complicated loco kits on the market, which match anything in terms of quality that can be said about top-end kits for standard gauge prototypes, it is true that most folk dip their toes into narrow gauge modelling by modifying a proprietary locomotive with a cab of enlarged dimensions to suit the new scale.

Equally, kits and conversion parts are legion, to aid those who wish to leave the shores of 'opening the box' and actually try some creative modelling of their own. As many choose to model a freelance narrow gauge line, then as long as the finished result is plausible, no-one can say "it's wrong". As we have mentioned previously, this freedom is itself one of the great attractions of narrow gauge modelling.

We present here a distillation of some suitable projects which have appeared in RAILWAY MODELLER over the years, to tempt you into making a start with your own versions.

A starter loco for OO9

Established OO9 modellers are well-seasoned in the art of exploiting proprietary N gauge mechanisms to create all manner of British outline narrow gauge locomotives. Bachmann's N gauge 'Plymouth' 0-6-0 switcher (ref.60051) – which features a basic, but robust, mechanism – has long been a popular choice, forming the basis of many OO9 locomotives.

The aim with this model – constructed by Craig Tiley – was to produce a locomotive with the flavour of a small British diesel. It should be noted that, in reality, four-wheel diesels were far more common, especially in the smaller gauges. However, the beauty of the freelance approach is that, within reason, anything can be justified!

An alternative conversion project utilising the Bachmann 'Plymouth' model can be achieved using the range of etched body kits produced by A1 Models, which are available from Dundas Models.

Building the model

1

The Bachmann model features a robust split-chassis mechanism with cast sideframe detail. The body is held in position by two lugs cast on the chassis – one either side – which protrude through the plastic body moulding. Removal is just a case of easing the body sides away from the lugs using a small flat screwdriver.

2

A fine-toothed razor saw was used to remove the upper part of the moulded cab. The moulded detail on the remaining lower cab sides was sanded off to provide a smooth surface for attaching the replacement cab side sheets. The exhaust on top of the bonnet was also removed at this stage.

3

The parts for the replacement cab were cut out from a sheet of 20thou styrene. Each cab side comprises two pieces which are laminated together, thus strengthening the assembly and allowing the cab door to be modelled in relief. Note the larger cab window apertures of the inner sides which will form a rebate for the glazing. The front and back pieces were deliberately kept oversize so they could be trimmed to fit later on.

4

The new cab sides were attached using superglue and checked with a square to ensure everything was in line. Note how the lower edges of the windows have been positioned to clear the top of the part of the chassis that occupies the cab.

5

A small file was used to achieve the curved profile of the cab front and back pieces, prior to fitting them into rebates created in the edges of the sides. The front section was fitted by offering it up to the model and gradually removing material until it sat over the bonnet. Note how the back section has been cut to 'sit' on part of the original Plymouth shunter bodywork.

6

With the basic cab assembly in place, attention could be turned to adding the smaller details such as handrails and door handles. The holes were drilled out using a pin vice with a small bit. The handrails were fabricated from lengths of fine brass wire, bent into corners at each end using pliers and fixed in position using small spots of superglue. When fitting each handrail, a small scrap of 20thou styrene sheet was used as a temporary spacer between it and the bodyside.

9 I painted the locomotive prior to adding the glazing and roof. Humbrol acrylics were used, hand brushed using a small brush. The main green body colour (ref.RC409) required three coats to achieve a satisfactory coverage. To weather the locomotive I started by dry-brushing the detail with a light greyish brown colour, mixed from diluted Humbrol acrylic paints. I then used small amounts of Humbrol weathering powders to create a suitably work-worn and dusty appearance.

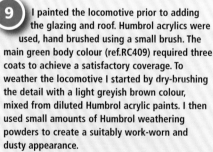

7

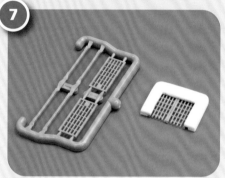

A new radiator was made to sit flush against the front of the original one on the Bachmann body. The housing was formed of two pieces of 40thou styrene sheet, laminated together with the edges then sanded to a rounded finish. The grille was created using a pair of Peco 4mm scale TPWS grids (ref.SL-46), cut to size.

10

Glazing for each window was cut from clear plastic sheet, fettled to fit and held in place using sparing amounts of impact adhesive. (Don't use liquid polystyrene as it is likely to 'frost' the glazing.) A cab roof was cut from 20thou styrene sheet, sized to create a small overhang on all four sides. It was formed into a curve by gently easing it around the shaft of a screwdriver in hot water and then immediately immersing in cold water to fix its shape. A driver was added using a Dapol plastic figure, chopped mid-torso to allow for the chassis which occupies much of the space in the cab.

8

Handrails were also added along the bonnet top, as illustrated, to help disguise the outline of the original model. The exhaust was fabricated using a section of brass wire inserted through some narrow brass tube. The strapping was cut from a self-adhesive label, just wrapped around the outside of the tube. The radiator filler cap is a Peco track pin, cut short and seated in a shallow pre-drilled hole with superglue. I chose at this point to beef up the buffer beams by removing the original moulded detail and adding overlays cut from 40thou styrene sheet.

11

A photo of the finished model, coupled to two Peco ready-to-run wagons, which were also weathered using the techniques described in Step 9. The couplings on the locomotive are the same as those fitted to the L&B stock (but with the loops removed), fixed in place by supergluing them into the existing coupling housings on the Bachmann chassis, reinforced with small sections of styrene strip.

Glyn Valley Tramway 4-Ton open wagon (ref.DM39)

Roger Christian demonstrates how plastic kits from the Dundas Models stable can offer a straightforward means of assembling a collection of 4mm narrow gauge rolling stock.

1 Small four-wheel open wagons were a staple of many narrow gauge railways, so this Dundas kit is suited to freelance applications as well as models depicting the GVT. The kit comprises just a handful of injection moulded components, together with a plastic load and narrow gauge 'curly spoked' wheels with metal tyres.

The assembly sequence is very straightforward, almost rendering the instructions supplied obsolete, but reference to them can be helpful if only to check the parts. Start by fixing one end onto the floor, using the try square or wooden block to ensure the parts are at right angles.

Next add one side followed by the opposite side. The corners are mitred to give a good joint, so apply the solvent only to the inside of each corner, then turn the body over carefully and run the solvent along the underside of the floor/side joins as above.

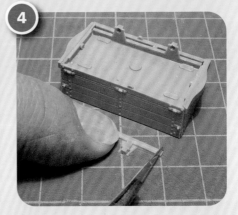

Add the other end and leave to cure for a while. Remove the solebars from the sprue and trim equal amounts of both ends so that they fit just inside the ends of the wagon. Cement only one of them in place first, ensuring it fits and sets square in all planes.

Follow the final stages of the instructions and fit the brake handles. As the model is bottom-heavy, it will not stand on its side without toppling over, so I use a small stepped wooden block to keep it on its side whilst the brake gear is fitted. The wagon is complete.

Using the other solebar, hold one axle in position and check it fits at right angles and rotates freely. Tack cement the end of the solebar and leave for a couple of minutes before springing in the second axle, then cement the solebar fully in position.

7 The completed model, ready for painting and finishing in the chosen livery. It is posed alongside a freelance van (based on a GVT prototype), also available from Dundas Models.

With a full system of trackwork for this scale/gauge combination available from Peco, 7mm narrow gauge offers a fascinating alternative for railway modellers seeking a model-building project a little off-the-beaten-track. Although no ready-to-run items are presently on the market for UK-outline locos, wagons and coaches in O-16.5, there are dozens of very useful kits available in a variety of materials.

David Malton shows how to construct a plastic kit from the Peco range, adding a few personal touches along the way; whilst the modular range of coach sides marketed by Peco for this scale is demonstrated with a vehicle constructed by the late Howard E S Clarke.

Peco four-wheel coach kit (ref.OR-32)

1

The Peco kit is simple to build, and does not necessarily require any painting. It is loosely based on the Glyn Valley Tramway prototypes, but I have chosen to adapt it slightly to suit my tastes and add a few extra details such as interior fittings. The guard's lookouts are optional and simply fit into one of the window openings.

2

The first job was adding the details to each side, which is easiest done before assembly. I deviated from the instructions here, and chose to cut and fit individual bits of glazing to each window, closer to the outer surface of the coach.

3

The end steps and handrail are part of the kit, but I also added lamp irons from bits of scrap brass. To make more of a feature of the guard's compartment, I cut an extra window in this end and added top and bottom frames for it from plastic strip.

4

The sides are glued to the outside edges of the ends, otherwise the floor won't fit properly later. This is easy to get wrong, and if so, will need correcting before moving on.

5

The brake rigging parts need a spacer, which I made from scraps of plasticard, to align them properly with the wheels. Since continuous brakes are a legal requirement on passenger trains these days, I also added a spare vacuum brake cylinder and pipes left over from another project. I used the couplings that came with the kit, but a more functional alternative could be fitted with modification to the buffer beams.

6

A simple interior was made from plasticard. It is not super-detailed, but enough to create an impression when viewed through the windows. An important addition was the partition to divide the interior into two compartments.

7

Only one lamp cover is supplied with the kit, but in my chosen brake coach configuration, with two separate compartments, another one was needed. I built a copy of the original out of plastic tube and plasticard, and glued it on the centreline of the roof (inset). A tail lamp and paint job on the ends and chassis are the finishing touches to the model. Although the gloss finish of the pre-printed sides looks nice, it's a bit too shiny for my liking, so I toned it down with Humbrol Matt Cote and subtle dry brush weathering.

A bogie coach from Peco modular components

Individual coach side sections are available in the Peco O-16.5 range, which allow a seemingly infinite number of different coach sides to be created; the only limitations being your imagination and the size of vehicle that your layout can accommodate! These sections comprise individual coach doors (ref.OR-50), coach panels (ref.OR-51), double-window coach panels (ref.OR-52), saloon window coach panels (ref.OR-53), coach window glazing (ref.OR-54), coach window blanks (ref.OR-55) and duckets (ref.OR-56).

It should be noted that any two parts from ref.OR-50 or ref.OR-51 equals one part from OR-52 or OR-53. All the sections have top-light windows; a pair of locating lugs to connect up to the next piece and a 1mm groove in the rear into which slots the floor.

To complete a sheet of 40thou styrene is needed for the floor and ends, running boards/steps, interior compartment partitions, seats and the roof, all cut to the width of the desired loading gauge. (No ends, roof or underframe details are available in the Peco range, thereby allowing the individual modeller to decide on the gauge and width of their coaches.) Door handles, roof ventilators and lamp tops are available from the 7mm Narrow Gauge Association, although suitable 7mm standard gauge items can be used, available from suppliers including Slater's.

A coach built using these parts is illustrated here, equipped with Ratio diamond frame bogies (ref.125) fitted with Bachmann 12mm diameter wheelsets.

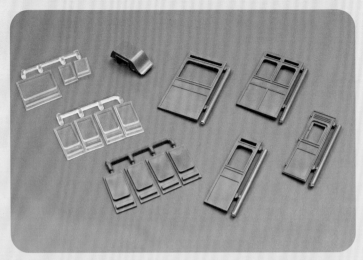

Illustrated here is the range of Peco coach parts; the panels and doors are each sold in packs of six whilst the windows come in packs of seven, window blanks in packs of eight and duckets in packs of four.

This vehicle is a five-compartment all-third, finished in a livery similar to that of the original L&B. The coach was built as part of a fixed rake of four, with the other vehicles having different side layouts to suit different coach types.

A view of the end of one of the coach ends. The roof profile and width mirrors that of the Peco four-wheel coach kit.

The modular components laid out to show what was required to form the sides for the model. Being a symmetrical design, both sides share the same configuration.

The underside of the coach showing the Ratio bogies fixed directly to the floor. Note how the bogies face inwards so that the coupling bosses do not foul the Kadee couplings.

Building locos for O-16.5

Although there are no proprietary locomotive models currently available for O-16.5, a good range of kits exist, including a trio of whitemetal body kits from Peco. These comprise a Quarry Hunslet 0-4-0ST (below), a Fletcher Jennings 0-4-2T, and a Glyn Valley Tramway Beyer Peacock 0-4-2T (with enclosed wheels and motion). All the kits can be obtained with a corresponding Branchlines chassis kit, wheels and motor, although they are of etched construction and *require soldered assembly. However, the Glyn Valley Tramway 0-4-2T kit can easily be modified to take a proprietary mechanism, such as the example illustrated (inset) which utilises a Hornby 'Smokey Joe' chassis. This particular kit is therefore well suited to modellers with lesser experience, as the body can be glued together using epoxy resin or superglue.*

The main focus of this feature is the Quarry Hunslet body kit (re.OL-3) and chassis kit (ref.BL-1), constructed by David Malton and previously described in the September and October 2013 issues of RAILWAY MODELLER.

Constructing the chassis

1

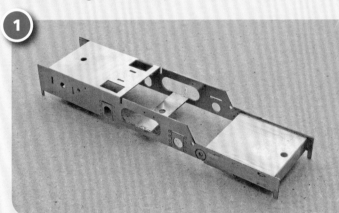

With loco construction projects it is best practice to start construction with the chassis, because it is easier to fettle the body to fit the chassis rather than the other way around. The first task is to fold and solder the chassis etch, ensuring everything is square. A 'V' shaped piece of nickel silver on the underside of the chassis (inset) provides a basic means of compensation for the front axle.

2

3 The motor and gearbox were assembled and made to work separate from the loco. The gearbox is a folded etched part with brass bearings soldered in. The gears were held on to the axles with grub screws; the assembly was then tested on its own (inset) before being partially dismantled to enable the inside of the chassis and wheels to be painted. The wheelsets and motor/gearbox assembly were then fitted to the chassis; the wheels were a push fit onto the axles and needed fixing in place with a small touch of superglue.

The main structure of the cylinders is a simple 'U' shape with a lost wax brass casting soldered on. The outer cover is purely cosmetic and was added later once all was working properly. It was important to get the cast slide in correct alignment with the cylinder for smooth running later on. The piston rod castings needed smoothing with fine sandpaper to allow them to pass easily through the slide.

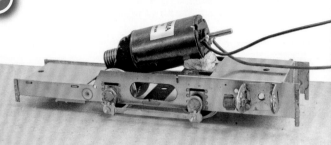

Each crank was made up from a laminate of two etched parts fitted to a top-hat bearing. The cranks were then attached to the axle ends, again using superglue. I attached one side first (together with the coupling rods), and then adjusted the other side until the chassis ran smoothly with no tight spots.

Next the connecting rods were attached to the crossheads and slidebars; a paper washer prevented the two parts from being inadvertently soldered together (inset). The chassis, cranks and rods were then painted prior to final assembly. The tiny nuts that go on the end of the crankpins required a small dab of glue to prevent them working loose.

All that remained was to fabricate the pickups as shown. The wire used and the bit of PC board were supplied with the kit, and the assembly was bolted on through the hole in the middle stretcher. The last stage was to run the mechanism in once the bearings, crankpins and slidebars has been lubricated with thin model oil.

Constructing the body

Superglue was used for the assembly of the body, but low-melt solder could be used if preferred. The first task was to build the running plate, front buffer beam and cab rear, this assembly then being fettled where required to achieve a good fit with the chassis.

The saddle tank and smokebox were built up as individual sub-assemblies and were trial-fitted to the running plate and buffer beam assembly on the chassis. Some material needed removing from the locating tabs of the saddle tank before it would fit properly over the motor. A square was used to align the chimney. Filler was used to hide gaps between adjoining parts, such as this seam along the saddle tank (inset).

Building locos for O-16.5

The cab front and sides are added next, followed by the saddle tank and smokebox assemblies. The photo shows the roof placed in position – it being removable to allow the installation and painting of cab details (inset). Other external details have also been added, including sandboxes and the safety valve.

Five brass handrail knobs are supplied in the kit and corresponding dimples in the castings show where to position them. I drilled out the holes using a pin vice and used a spare length of wire to hold and position the four knobs on the tank sides, to ensure they were fitted level, before fixing in place with superglue. The wire for the rail was curved to shape using a Humbrol paint tin. The fifth knob that attaches to the chimney was then threaded onto the wire loose, and then the wire was threaded through the knobs on the tank sides. I then trimmed off the excess wire between the rearward knobs and cab front, a bit at a time, until both sides were equal and the handrail was in the correct position.

A representation of the injector pipework was added to finish, and then the body was washed in warm soapy water to remove any debris and grease prior to painting. When dry, the body was sprayed with grey primer to give the paint an even surface to adhere to. The primer also highlighted any blemishes that required smoothing out prior to applying the top coat.

To complete, a set of custom made etched brass name and works plates were fitted, made by Narrow Planet. Tension-lock couplings were fitted for the time being, glued into the slots in the buffer beams. I glued real coal into the bunkers in the cab, and finally applied some subtle weathering to the whole loco.

The loco was painted in its 'as preserved' maroon livery using Humbrol enamel, with acrylic used for the black parts. The brass fittings were painted using Humbrol metallic finish gold paint and then the whole model was treated to a coat of satin varnish. It was lined out using a Fox Transfers lining sheet, with the model supported in a Peco loco servicing cradle.

SUBSCRIBE
AND GET THE VERY BEST IN

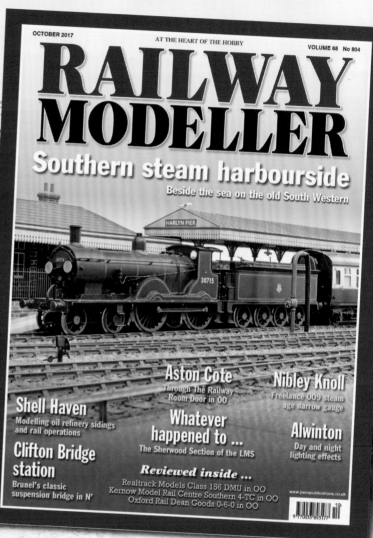

OCTOBER 2017　　AT THE HEART OF THE HOBBY　　VOLUME 68　No 804

RAILWAY MODELLER

Southern steam harbourside
Beside the sea on the old South Western

Aston Cote
Through The Railway Room Door in OO

Nibley Knoll
Freelance OO9 steam age narrow gauge

Shell Haven
Modelling oil refinery sidings and rail operations

Whatever happened to ...
The Sherwood Section of the LMS

Alwinton
Day and night lighting effects

Clifton Bridge station
Brunel's classic suspension bridge in N'

Reviewed inside ...
Realtrack Models Class 156 DMU in OO
Kernow Model Rail Centre Southern 4-TC in OO
Oxford Rail Dean Goods 0-6-0 in OO

www.pecopublications.co.uk

PLUS!

Chapter 7

Building a narrow gauge layout

Broadly speaking the construction of a narrow gauge railway is not much different from modelling a standard gauge subject; the fundamental stages of baseboard construction, track laying, wiring and scenery are the same. However, capturing the character of a narrow gauge prototype requires something of a lighter touch and – for some aspects – a slightly different approach from that for standard gauge systems.

The subject of this article is a freelance OO9 layout that has been constructed by members

Above and left
Two views of the finished model, which between them illustrate the entire scenic section for the side under construction. Shown to good effect is the multi-level running lines, with the standard gauge along the back. The articulated railcar (painted blue and cream) is a freelance design built from spare Peco L&B coach mouldings and powered by a Kato 11-103 mechanism. The Manning Wardle 2-6-2T is a Backwoods Miniatures etched kit.

of the Peco product deisgn team (David Malton and Bob Phelps) for display at exhibitions. It occupies an area of 8' x 3', with a central backscene running along the length of the layout, thereby splitting it into two scenic halves. There is a dual-level narrow gauge system, comprising of a continuous run on the lower level, together with a branch shuttle that runs from a station on the lower level and climbs up and round, through to a high level station on the other side. There is also a standard gauge line (OO) that runs at a higher level along one side only.

This article focuses specifically on the side of the layout with the standard gauge line, which has been inspired by the many preserved systems that can be found around the United Kingdom. It has been constructed almost exclusively using products from the Peco Group range, but some other items and materials have been used where required, as identified in the step-by-step captions.

BUILDING THE LAYOUT

1 Baseboards and scenic sub-base

The layout comprises three baseboard sections (to aid portability), built from timber with open frames to keep overall weight to a minimum. Boards are aligned using EM Gauge Society joiners, and case catches are used to lock them together. The baseboard surfaces were covered with panels of 2" thick insulating polystyrene, a second tier added to provide the basis of the higher level. Note the wooden profiles for the board ends at the intermediate joins. The trackwork (a plan was devised with the aid of Anyrail™ software prior to construction) was then drawn out, with cork underlay fixed in place using a high strength DIY adhesive. Points are placed in position to check the geometry, with items of stock being used to check clearances and siding lengths.

2 Creating the graded section of running line

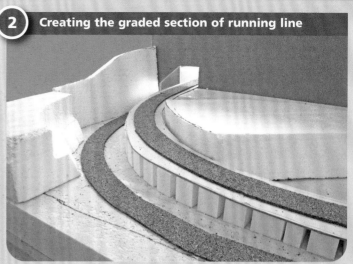

The layout features a narrow gauge line that climbs from the lower level station up and round to a higher level on the other scenic side. The foundation for the graded part of this line was achieved using a Woodland Scenics kit; the 4% Incline/Decline set (ref.ST1411), which raises the height of the trackbed by 4" over a distance of 8'. The kit uses sections made from high-density foam, which can be curved to suit the desired track geometry. It is very easy to use and allows a constant gradient to be achieved with the minimum of fuss. A layer of card was added to provide a smooth trackbed surface, onto which the cork underlay was fixed. Incline sets for shallower and steeper gradients are also available.

3 Laying the track

The plain narrow gauge track was laid using Peco OO9 flexible track (ref.SL-400, irregular sleeper type), together with small radius Peco Electrofrog points (ref.SL-E491 left and ref.SLE492 right). Track was fixed to the cork underlay using impact adhesive, with drawing pins used to hold the track *in situ* whilst the adhesive dried. The inset picture shows how plain track was laid across the board joins, with small sections of the sleeper base removed to allow the rails to be soldered to the heads of brass screws. (The screws were inserted before laying the track.) The rails were then cut through after soldering, thus preventing the rail ends from springing back. This arrangement at board joins ensures good track alignment each time the layout is set up.

4 Developing the locomotive shed and yard

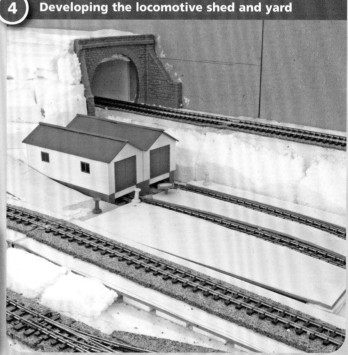

The narrow gauge engine shed was made by combining two Wills Station Garage kits (ref.SS12), with a brick plinth added to increase the height to accommodate the locomotives. This exemplifies how, with some ingenuity, kits can be adapted for use on a narrow gauge railway. Thin card was used for the shed yard to inset the track. This view also shows how expanded polystyrene (of the type commonly used for packaging) was used to form the scenery. A hot wire cutter was used to trim pieces to the required shapes.

5 Adding the scenic outer shell and ballasting

Peco Landform (ref.PS–36) was used to cover the areas of expanded polystyrene and provide a solid scenic outer shell. The rail sides were then painted using Humbrol enamels to give them a realistic dark brown appearance. Once dry, ballasting of the track was undertaken, using Peco Scene Fine Grade Grey Stone – clean (ref.PS-300).

6 Modelling a girder bridge

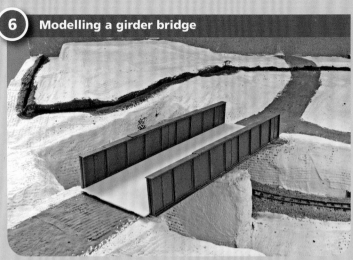

The bridge was constructed using the Wills Varigirder bridge spans kit (ref.SS57) and a plasticard road deck. Note the removable section of scenery behind the bridge, which is required to allow access to the hidden parts of the running lines should the need arise. The edges of this section have been painted a dark earth colour to help disguise them once the grass and vegetation is added.

7 Station detailing

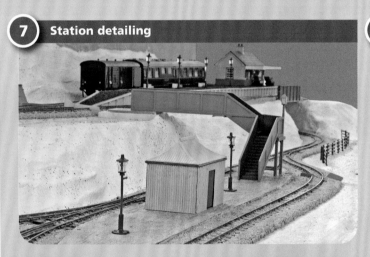

Low platforms were a common feature of passenger-carrying narrow gauge railways. This island platform was fabricated from balsa, with lamps from the Modelscene range (ref.5004) and a Wills GWR style Pagoda hut (ref.SS35) serving as a shelter. The footbridge, which connects the narrow gauge platform with the high level standard gauge line, is a modified Ratio SR Concrete Footbridge kit (ref.517).

8 Rendering rock faces and applying the grass

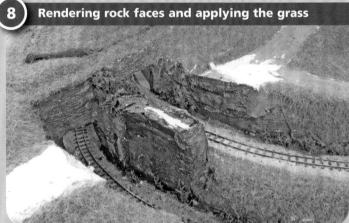

Rock faces were rendered by adding a thin layer of DIY filler to the Peco Landform outer shell, the texture being created using a small piece of styrene sheet. The area was then covered in a very dark grey colour, with lighter shades dry-brushed over the top to highlight the surface texture. DIY filler was also used to create the road surfaces. The grass areas of scenery were covered using static grass from the Peco Scene range, applied on a thin layer of Basing glue.

9 Fencing, hedges and trees

Trees and hedges were added from the K&M range, whilst fencing was added using Peco Lineside Flexible Fencing (ref.LK-45). Peco Fine Grade Sand (ref.PS-344) was used for the road surfaces, with K&M scatter used to simulate patches of grass running along the middle. Other scatters and clump foliage were used to create bushes and shrubs.

11 Lineside clutter

Lineside clutter is a common feature of locomotive sheds, even in narrow gauge. Many railways had obsolete or decaying locomotives dumped by the lineside, and this has been replicated here using a Peco whitemetal body kit (ref.GL-1) for a freelance narrow gauge steam locomotive, with some strategically placed vegetation to hide the fact that it doesn't have a chassis! The canvas sheeting over the chimney was made using tissue, coated in PVA and allowed to dry solid, and then painted to suit. Corroded surfaces were simulated using Modelmates Rust Effect paint. The standard gauge container is from the Modelscene range (ref.5010), whilst the grounded coach body is a Ratio kit (ref.501).

10 Creating the river

The channel for the river was carved into the insulated polystyrene at an earlier stage of the project. The river bed itself was created (inset) using a combination of Peco Scene materials; Limestone – medium (ref.PS-342) and Limestone – coarse (ref.PS-343). The water was added using Woodland Scenics Realistic Water (ref.C1211), which can be poured directly from the bottle and is self-levelling. Further detailing was added using more of the Peco Limestone granules, together with sand for the bank and Woodland Scenics fibres for the reeds.

12 A photographic backscene

A backscene was the final scenic addition to the layout, created using a landscape stitched together digitally from a series of photographs and then sized and printed to suit. The transition between the edge of the layout scenery and the backscene was disguised with the addition of hedges from the K&M range. Photographic backscenes are available 'off the shelf' from a number of model railway retailers.

Chapter 8

Narrow gauge layout plans

All fired up and ready to make a start at building your first narrow gauge layout? To help you along the way, we have assembled, in this final section, a small collection of layout plans for OO9 and O-16.5 gauges, most of which have previously been designed and/or built by experienced narrow gauge modellers.

Remember that the methods, techniques and skills necessary for building a narrow gauge layout are little different from those for other gauges, and all the accessories and kits available in your chosen scale are equally useful, so you should not come across any real difficulties or insurmountable obstacles to hold you up.

Here's to narrow gauge railway modelling!

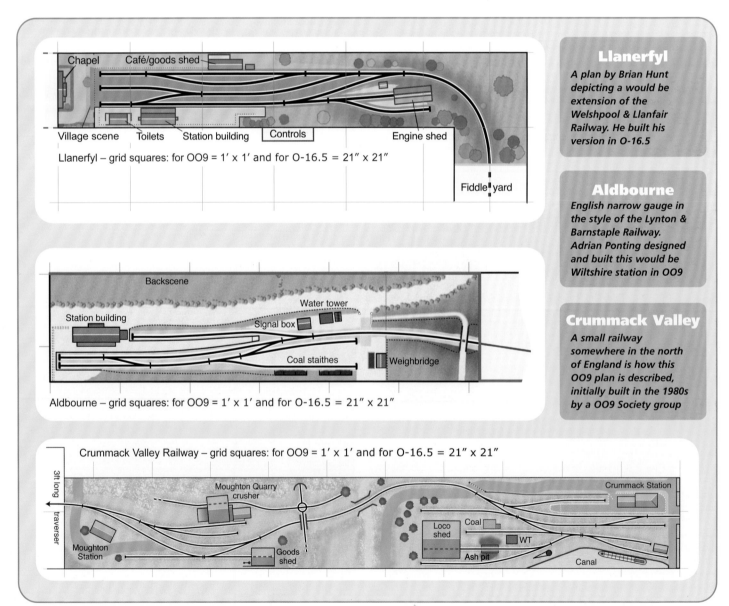

Llanerfyl – grid squares: for OO9 = 1' x 1' and for O-16.5 = 21" x 21"

Aldbourne – grid squares: for OO9 = 1' x 1' and for O-16.5 = 21" x 21"

Crummack Valley Railway – grid squares: for OO9 = 1' x 1' and for O-16.5 = 21" x 21"

Llanerfyl
A plan by Brian Hunt depicting a would be extension of the Welshpool & Llanfair Railway. He built his version in O-16.5

Aldbourne
English narrow gauge in the style of the Lynton & Barnstaple Railway. Adrian Ponting designed and built this would be Wiltshire station in OO9

Crummack Valley
A small railway somewhere in the north of England is how this OO9 plan is described, initially built in the 1980s by a OO9 Society group

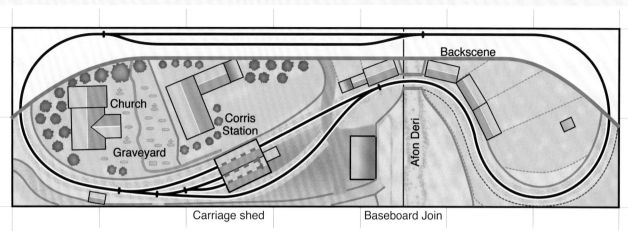

Corris – grid squares: for OO9 = 1' x 1' and for O-16.5 = 21" x 21"

Corris

Rod Alcock's interpretation of this classic Welsh narrow gauge railway station. Built to OO9 standards and featuring aspects of the village structures, it occupies a space of 7' x 2'. Although a strict scale replica of the location it conveniently doubles as a continuous run layout for exhibitions

Torreton

A continuous run layout in OO9 that packs a lot of operational interest into just 3'3" x 2'3". Built by Lyn and Jim Owers it depicts an iron ore mine in Leicestershire, where once many similar mining and quarrying operations were served by narrow gauge networks. Note that the fiddle yard loops are spaced widely apart so as to ensure sufficient clearance between adjacent rakes of stock

Castle Wharf

In the style and genre of English narrow gauge again with this layout portraying a might have been Colonel Stephens line in Cumbria. Built as an exhibition layout to OO9 standards by Ian Kirkwood, the layout has a metric 'footprint' of 1200mm (3'11") x 500mm (1'8")

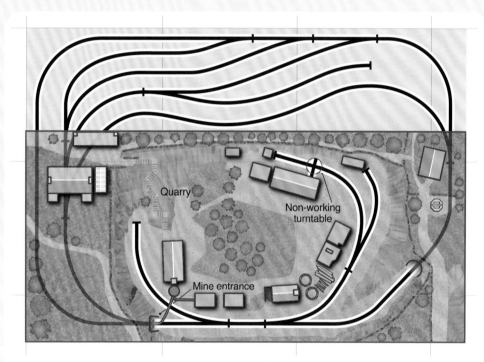

Torreton – grid squares: for OO9 = 1' x 1' and for O-16.5 = 21" x 21"

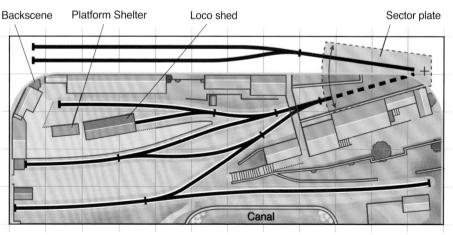

Castle Wharf – grid squares: for OO9 = 100mm x 100mm, for O-16.5 = 175mm x 175mm

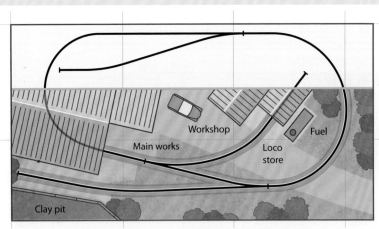

United Brick and Clay Works – grid squares: for OO9 = 1' x 1' and for O-16.5 = 21" x 21"

United Brick and Clay Works

Demonstrating that you can squeeze a lot of scenic and operating interest onto a small baseboard in O-16.5.
United Brick and Clay Works was built by Julian Andrews as his first venture into 7mm narrow gauge modelling. The buildings cleverly disguise the fact that the track is actually arranged as a continuous run – ideal for exhibition purposes when taking one's lunch!

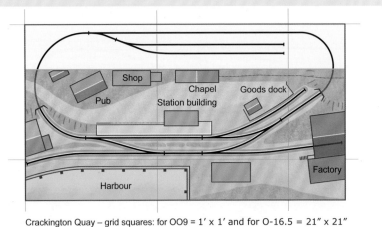

Crackington Quay – grid squares: for OO9 = 1' x 1' and for O-16.5 = 21" x 21"

Crackington Quay

Another small 7mm narrow gauge layout including a harbour scene in just 51" x 27". Built by Roy Parkes, almost everything was derived from kits or scratch, making O-16.5 very much a true 'modellers' scale. This is one of the reasons why an awful lot of enthusiasts choose narrow gauge as a way of enjoying the traditional skills of the hobby

Acknowledgements

Thanks are due to the following, whose modelling made this book possible. Sadly, some are no longer with us.

Rod Allcock; David Atkinson; Andrew & Joseph Beard; David Burleigh; members of the Burnley Model Railway Club; Alan Catlow; Roger Christian; Nick Colthorpe; Ken Ellworthy; Bryan Fryer; David Gander; Alan Gee; John Green; Ian Gurr; P D Hancock; James Hilton; Peter Hollins; members of the Hull Miniature Railway Society; Gareth Jones; Peter Kazer; Richard Lane; Howard & Eileen Lawrence; Peter Leadley; David Lenton; David Malton; David Mander; Warren Miller; Tony Morris; Graham Morfoot; Derek Naylor; Roger Nicholls; members of the Norton Cross Model Railway Group; Hugh Norwood; Jim & Lyn Owers; Bob Phelps; Ted Polet; Davide Raseni; Stuart Reeves; Ian Roberts; Diger Rossel; Keith Skillicorn; Ulrich Slovig; David Taylor; Paul Titmuss; John Thorne; Tim Tincknell; members of the Trent Valley Group of the 7mm NGA; Rocerik Vanderkelen; members of the Wakefield Railway Modellers' Society; Angus Watkins; Daniel James Wells; Matt Wildsmith; James Williams; Stan Williams; Paul Windle; and David Woodcock.

Bibliography

Lost Lines – British Narrow Gauge
by Nigel Welbourn
Published by Ian Allan
ISBN 0-7110-2742-0

The Glyn Valley Tramway
by W J Milner
Published by Oxford Publishing Co.
ISBN 0 86093 286 9

**The Narrow Gauge Charm of Yesterday
– A Pictorial Tribute**
by Ivo Peters
Published by Oxford Publishing Co.
ISBN 0 902888 65 X

The Vale of Rheidol Light Railway
by C C Green
Published by Wild Swan Publications
ISBN 0 906867 43 6

The Modeller Book of Narrow Gauge
Edited by David Lloyd
Published by Peco Publications
ISBN 0-900586-00-1

**The Isle of Man Railway
– A Modeller's Inspiration**
by Robin G Winter
Published by Peco Publications
ISBN 978-0900586958

**The Isle of Man Railway – Colour photographs
1963 – 1971**
by Eric E Bird
Published by Peco Publications
ISBN 978-0900586439

**The Isle of Man Railway – 1950s photographs
by David Odabashian** by Robin G Winter
Published by Peco Publications
ISBN 978-0900586392

Modelling the Irish Narrow Gauge
by David Lloyd
Published by Peco Publications
ISBN 0 900586 15 X